Kaplan Publishing are constantly finding new ways to make a difference to your studies and our exciting online resources really do offer something different to students looking for exam success.

This book comes with free MyKaplan online resources so that you can study anytime, anywhere. **This free online resource is not sold separately and is included in the price of the book.**

Having purchased this book, you have access to the following online study materials:

CONTENT	AAT	
	Text	Kit
iPaper version of the book	✓	✓
Progress tests with instant answers	✓	
Mock assessments online	✓	✓
Material updates	✓	✓

D0486829

How to access your online resources

Kaplan Financial students will already have a MyKaplan account and these extra resources will be available to you online. You do not need to register again, as this process was completed when you enrolled. If you are having problems accessing online materials, please ask your course administrator.

If you are already a registered MyKaplan user go to www.MyKaplan.co.uk and log in. Select the 'add a book' feature and enter the ISBN number of this book and the unique pass key at the bottom of this card. Then click 'finished' or 'add another book'. You may add as many books as you have purchased from this screen.

If you purchased through Kaplan Flexible Learning or via the Kaplan Publishing website you will automatically receive an e-mail invitation to MyKaplan. Please register your details using this email to gain access to your content. If you do not receive the e-mail or book content, please contact Kaplan Flexible Learning.

If you are a new user register at www.MyKaplan.co.uk and click on the link contained in the email we sent you to activate your account. Then select the 'add a book' feature, enter the ISBN number of this book and the unique pass key at the bottom of this card. Then click 'finished' or 'add another book'.

Your Code and Information

This code can only be used once for the registration of one book online. This registration and your online content will expire when the final sittings for the examinations covered by this book have taken place. Please allow one hour from the time you submit your book details for us to process your request.

Please scratch the film to access your MyKaplan code.

Please be aware that this code is case-sensitive and you will need to include the dashes within the passcode, but not when entering the ISBN. For further technical support, please visit www.MyKaplan.co.uk

AQ2013 Level 2

Control Accounts, Journals and the Banking System

REVISION KIT

British Library Cataloguing-in-Publication Data

A catalogue record for this book is available from the British Library.

Published by:

Kaplan Publishing UK

Unit 2 The Business Centre

Molly Millar's Lane

Wokingham

Berkshire

RG41 2QZ

ISBN: 978-1-78415-352-6

© Kaplan Financial Limited, 2015

Printed and bound in Great Britain.

CONTENTS

	Page
Index to questions and answers	v
Exam technique	ix
Paper specific information	xi
Kaplan's recommended revision approach	xiii

Features in this exam kit

In addition to providing a wide ranging bank of real exam style questions, we have also included in this kit:

- Paper specific information and advice on exam technique.

- Our recommended approach to make your revision for this particular subject as effective as possible.

You will find a wealth of other resources to help you with your studies on the AAT website:

www.aat.org.uk/

Quality and accuracy are of the utmost importance to us so if you spot an error in any of our products, please send an email to mykaplanreporting@kaplan.com with full details, or follow the link to the feedback form in MyKaplan.

Our Quality Co-ordinator will work with our technical team to verify the error and take action to ensure it is corrected in future editions

INDEX TO QUESTIONS AND ANSWERS

		Page number	
		Question	Answer
THE JOURNAL			
1	Intrepid Interiors	1	75
2	Bedroom Bits	2	75
3	Garden Gates	2	76
PAYROLL			
4	Ivano	3	76
5	Anna	3	77
6	Gross Pay 1	4	77
7	Gross Pay 2	4	78
8	A Pocket Full of Poses	5	78
9	Rhyme Time	6	79
10	Down & Out	7	80
11	Dev's	8	80
IRRECOVERABLE DEBTS, CONTRAS AND TYPES OF ERROR			
12	Bedroom Bits 2	9	81
13	Garden Gates 2	9	81
14	Chestnut	9	82
15	Allen	10	82
16	Error Types 1	11	83
17	Error Types 2	11	83
18	Error Types 3	12	84
19	Error Types 4	12	84
20	Error Type 5	12	84
21	Principles	13	84
22	Extraction	13	84
ERRORS			
23	Bank error	14	85
24	Rent error	14	85
25	Gas error	15	85
26	Buildings error	15	85
27	Sales error	15	86

		Page number	
		Question	Answer
BALANCING THE TRIAL BALANCE AND CORRECTION OF ERRORS			
28	CB Interiors	16	86
29	Roger Dodger	17	86
30	A Cut Above	18	87
31	Restco	19	87
32	Johnny Joiner	20	87
33	Buckley Drains	20	88
34	Mendonca	21	88
35	Beasant	21	88
POST JOURNAL ENTRIES TO LEDGER ACCOUNTS			
36	Pat's Cafe	22	89
37	Twinkle's Trinkets	23	90
38	Sparks and Mencer	25	91
39	Pirate Pete's	26	92
RE-DRAFT THE TRIAL BALANCE			
40	Rick's Racers	28	93
41	Percy Pots	29	94
42	Ivor Island	31	95
43	Ring of Roses	32	96
44	Hearn	33	97
45	Rodman	34	98
UPDATE THE CASH BOOK			
46	Rivers Ltd	36	99
47	Luxury Bathrooms	37	99
48	Wholesale Flooring	39	100
49	24 Hour Taxis	40	100
50	Wood	41	101
51	Pearson	42	101
52	McKeown	43	102
BANK RECONCILIATION			
53	Rivers Bank Reconciliation	44	102
54	Luxury Bathrooms Bank Reconciliation	45	103
55	Wholesale Flooring Bank Reconciliation	47	103
56	24 Hour Taxis Bank Reconciliation	48	103
57	Wood Bank Reconciliation	50	104
58	Pearson Bank Reconciliation	51	104
59	McKeown Bank Reconciliation	53	105

KAPLAN PUBLISHING

		Page number	
		Question	Answer
PREPARE AND RECONCILE SALES/PURCHASE LEDGER CONTROL ACCOUNTS			
60	Monster Munchies	54	105
61	Jack's Box	56	106
62	Cilla's Sinks	58	107
63	Vik's Tricks	59	108
64	Zhang	61	109
65	Handyside	62	110
VAT CONTROL ACCOUNT			
66	Benjamin Bishop	63	111
67	Ring Ring Telephone	64	111
68	Jo's Joiners	65	112
69	Philip's Cabins	66	112
70	Disley	67	112
71	Kerr	67	113
72	Neilson	68	113
THE BANKING SYSTEM			
73	Colbeck	68	114
74	Blossom Blooms	69	114
75	Bella Bakers	69	115
76	Pete's Parrots	70	115
77	Banks	71	116
78	Kite Ltd	72	117
79	Building Society	72	117
80	Gates	73	118
81	Methods of payment	74	119
82	Methods of payment 2	74	119

MOCK EXAM		
Questions	121	
Answers		135

EXAM TECHNIQUE

- **Do not skip any of the material** in the syllabus.

- **Read each question** *very* carefully.

- **Double-check your answer** before committing yourself to it.

- Answer **every** question – if you do not know an answer to a multiple choice question or true/false question, you don't lose anything by guessing. Think carefully before you **guess**.

- If you are answering a multiple-choice question, **eliminate first those answers that you know are wrong**. Then choose the most appropriate answer from those that are left.

- **Don't panic** if you realise you've answered a question incorrectly. Getting one question wrong will not mean the difference between passing and failing

Computer-based exams – tips

- Do not attempt a CBA until you have **completed all study material** relating to it.

- On the AAT website there is a CBA demonstration. It is **ESSENTIAL** that you attempt this before your real CBA. You will become familiar with how to move around the CBA screens and the way that questions are formatted, increasing your confidence and speed in the actual exam.

- Be sure you understand how to use the **software** before you start the exam. If in doubt, ask the assessment centre staff to explain it to you.

- Questions are **displayed on the screen** and answers are entered using keyboard and mouse. At the end of the exam, you are given a certificate showing the result you have achieved.

- In addition to the traditional multiple-choice question type, CBAs will also contain **other types of questions**, such as number entry questions, drag and drop, true/false, pick lists or drop down menus or hybrids of these.

- In some CBAs you will have to type in complete computations or written answers.

- You need to be sure you **know how to answer questions** of this type before you sit the exam, through practice.

TERMINOLOGY

The AAT fully adopted IFRS terminology on 1 January 2012. The IFRS terms do not impact greatly on the Control Accounts, Journals and the Banking Systems paper. The listing provided gives the IFRS term (AAT preferred term) and the related UK GAAP term. You should ensure you are familiar with the following terms:

UK GAAP	IFRS
Trade debtors/Debtors	Trade receivables/Receivables
Trade creditors/Creditors	Trade payables/Payables
Debtors ledger control account	Receivables ledger control account
Sales ledger control account	Sales ledger control account
Creditors ledger control account	Payables ledger control account
Purchases ledger control account	Purchases ledger control account
Sales/Purchases ledger	Sales/Purchases ledger
Sales tax/VAT	Sales tax/VAT
Fixed asset	Non-current asset
Stock	Inventory
Bad debt	Irrecoverable debt

Also note, under payroll the terms "PAYE" and "National Insurance Contributions (NIC)" may also be known as "Income Tax" and "Social Security" respectively.

DETAILED SYLLABUS

The detailed syllabus and study guide written by the AAT can be found at:

www.aat.org.uk/

PAPER SPECIFIC INFORMATION

THE EXAM

FORMAT OF THE ASSESSMENT

The CJBS assessment will last for 2 hours and will consist of 12 tasks. The task content is outlined below.

Task	Maximum marks	Title for topics within task range
1	12	Prepare journals for opening entries.
2	12	Prepare journals for payroll transactions.
3	14	Prepare journals for irrecoverable debts written off. Identify types of error.
4	12	Prepare journals for correction of errors.
5	12	Balance the trial balance and prepare journals for correction of errors.
6	12	Post journal entries to ledger accounts.
7	14	Redraft the trial balance.
8	14	Update the cash book.
9	14	Prepare a bank reconciliation statement.
10	14	Prepare and reconcile sales/purchase ledger accounts.
11	12	Prepare a VAT control account and verify the balance.
12	12	Understand the banking system and the importance of document retention.

PASS MARK

The pass mark for all AAT CBAs is 70%.

Always keep your eye on the clock and make sure you attempt all questions!

KAPLAN'S RECOMMENDED REVISION APPROACH

QUESTION PRACTICE IS THE KEY TO SUCCESS

Success in professional examinations relies upon you acquiring a firm grasp of the required knowledge at the tuition phase. In order to be able to do the questions, knowledge is essential.

However, the difference between success and failure often hinges on your exam technique on the day and making the most of the revision phase of your studies.

The **Kaplan textbook** is the starting point, designed to provide the underpinning knowledge to tackle all questions. However, in the revision phase, poring over text books is not the answer.

Kaplan pocket notes are designed to help you quickly revise a topic area; however you then need to practise questions. There is a need to progress to exam style questions as soon as possible, and to tie your exam technique and technical knowledge together.

The importance of question practice cannot be over-emphasised.

The recommended approach below is designed by expert tutors in the field, in conjunction with their knowledge of the examiner and the specimen assessment.

You need to practise as many questions as possible in the time you have left.

OUR AIM

Our aim is to get you to the stage where you can attempt exam questions confidently, to time, in a closed book environment, with no supplementary help (i.e. to simulate the real examination experience).

Practising your exam technique is also vitally important for you to assess your progress and identify areas of weakness that may need more attention in the final run up to the examination.

In order to achieve this we recognise that initially you may feel the need to practice some questions with open book help.

Good exam technique is vital.

THE KAPLAN CJBS REVISION PLAN

Stage 1: Assess areas of strengths and weaknesses

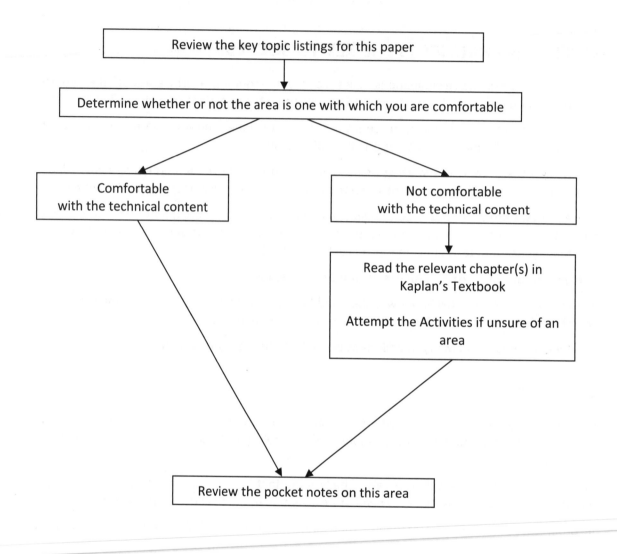

Review the key topic listings for this paper

Determine whether or not the area is one with which you are comfortable

Comfortable
with the technical content

Not comfortable
with the technical content

Read the relevant chapter(s) in
Kaplan's Textbook

Attempt the Activities if unsure of an
area

Review the pocket notes on this area

Stage 2: Practise questions

Follow the order of revision of topics as presented in this kit and attempt the questions in the order suggested.

Try to avoid referring to text books and notes and the model answer until you have completed your attempt.

Review your attempt with the model answer and assess how much of the answer you achieved.

| Comfortable with question attempt | Not comfortable with question attempts |

Focus on these areas by:

- Reworking Activities in Kaplan's Textbook/workbook

- Revisiting the technical content from Kaplan's pocket notes

- Working any remaining questions on that area in the exam kit

Only revisit when comfortable with questions on all topic areas

Stage 3: Final pre-exam revision

We recommend that you **attempt at least one mock examination** containing a set of previously unseen exam standard questions.

Attempt the mock CBA online in timed, closed book conditions to simulate the real exam experience.

Section 1

PRACTICE QUESTIONS

THE JOURNAL

1   INTREPID INTERIORS

Intrepid Interiors has started a new business, Intrepid Exteriors, and a new set of accounts are to be opened. A partially completed journal to record the opening entries is shown below.

Record the journal entries needed in the accounts in the general ledger of Intrepid Exteriors to deal with the opening entries.

Account name	Amount £	Debit ✓	Credit ✓
Cash at bank	7,250		
Bank loan	5,000		
Capital	10,625		
Motor vehicles	4,750		
Insurances	575		
Stationery	300		
Sundry expenses	225		
Motor expenses	135		
Advertising	990		
Rent and rates	1,400		
Journal to record the opening entries of new business			

2 BEDROOM BITS

Bedroom Bits has started a new business, Bedroom Bobs, and a new set of accounts are to be opened. A partially completed journal to record the opening entries is shown below.

Record the journal entries needed in the accounts in the general ledger of Bedroom Bobs to deal with the opening entries.

Account name	Amount £	Debit ✓	Credit ✓
Cash	325		
Cash at bank	9,625		
Capital	22,008		
Fixtures and fittings	4,250		
Insurance	1,050		
Loan from bank	15,000		
Miscellaneous expenses	413		
Motor vehicle	19,745		
Office expenses	350		
Rent and rates	1,250		
Journal to record the opening entries of new business			

3 GARDEN GATES

Garden Gates has started a new business, Garden Gnomes, and a new set of accounts are to be opened. A partially completed journal to record the opening entries is shown below.

Record the journal entries needed in the accounts in the general ledger of Garden Gnomes to deal with the opening entries.

Account name	Amount £	Debit ✓	Credit ✓
Cash	450		
Cash at bank	11,125		
Capital	28,941		
Plant and machinery	5,050		
Insurance	990		
Loan from bank	12,500		
General office expenses	378		
Motor vehicle	20,755		
Advertising	893		
Rent and rates	1,800		
Journal to record the opening entries of new business			

PAYROLL

4   IVANO

Ivano's pay details for June are listed below:

Transaction	Amount £
Gross pay	2,400
PAYE	480
Employee's NIC	245
Employee's contribution to pension	80
Employer's NIC	255

Fill in the boxes required below:

(a)

	Amount £
Net pay	

(b)

	Amount £
Wages and salaries (Employer's expense)	

(c)

	Amount £
Liabilities (HMRC and pension)	

5   ANNA

Anna's pay details for June are listed below:

Transaction	Amount £
Gross pay	1,400
PAYE	280
Employee's NIC	125
Employer's contribution to pension	70
Employee's contribution to pension	60
Employer's NIC	135

Fill in the boxes required below:

(a)

	Amount £
Net pay	

(b)

	Amount £
Wages and salaries (Employer's expense)	

(c)

	Amount £
Liabilities (HMRC and pension)	

6 GROSS PAY 1

Which of the items listed below would be classed as part of an employee's gross pay?

Item	Included in gross pay ✓	Not included in gross pay ✓
Salary		
Employer's NIC		
Overtime		
Bonus		
Expenses reimbursement		
PAYE		

7 GROSS PAY 2

Which of the items listed below would be classed as part of an employee's gross pay?

Item	Included in gross pay ✓	Not included in gross pay ✓
Salary		
Employer's NIC		
Commission		
Employee's NIC		
Pension contribution		
PAYE		

8   A POCKET FULL OF POSES

A Pocket Full of Poses pays its employees by cheque every month and maintains a wages control account. A summary of last month's payroll transactions is shown below:

Item	£
Gross wages	15,000
Employers' NI	1,755
Employees' NI	1,410
Income tax	4,335
Employer's pension contributions	1,000
Employee's pension contributions	850

Record the journal entries needed in the general ledger to:

(i)   **Record the wages expense**

(ii)   **Record the HM Revenue and Customs liability**

(iii)   **Record the net wages paid to the employees**

(iv)   **Record the pension liability**

(i)

Account name	Amount £	Debit ✓	Credit ✓

(ii)

Account name	Amount £	Debit ✓	Credit ✓

(iii)

Account name	Amount £	Debit ✓	Credit ✓

(iv)

Account name	Amount £	Debit ✓	Credit ✓

Picklist for each: Bank, Employees NI, Employers NI, HM Revenue and Customs, Income tax, Net wages, Pension, Trade union, Wages control, Wages expense.

9   RHYME TIME

Rhyme Time pays its employees by cheque every month and maintains a wages control account. A summary of last month's payroll transactions is shown below:

Item	£
Gross wages	10,130
Employers' NI	1,185
Employees' NI	1,006
Income tax	2,835
Employer's pension contributions	600
Employee's Pension contributions	550

Record the journal entries needed in the general ledger to:

(i)   **Record the wages expense**

(ii)   **Record the HM Revenue and Customs liability**

(iii) **Record the net wages paid to the employees**

(iv)   **Record the pension liability**

(i)

Account name	Amount £	Debit ✓	Credit ✓

(ii)

Account name	Amount £	Debit ✓	Credit ✓

(iii)

Account name	Amount £	Debit ✓	Credit ✓

(iv)

Account name	Amount £	Debit ✓	Credit ✓

10   DOWN & OUT

Down & Out pays it employees by cheque every month and maintains a wages control account. A summary of last month's payroll transactions is shown below:

Item	£
Gross wages	8,542
Employer's NI	1,025
Employees' NI	940
Income tax	1,708
Trade union fees	425

Record the journal entries needed in the general ledger to:

(i)   **Record the wages expense**

(ii)   **Record the HM Revenue & Customs liability**

(iii)   **Record the net wages paid to the employees**

(iv)   **Record the trade union liability**

(i)

Account name	Amount £	Debit ✓	Credit ✓

(ii)

Account name	Amount £	Debit ✓	Credit ✓

(iii)

Account name	Amount £	Debit ✓	Credit ✓

(iv)

Account name	Amount £	Debit ✓	Credit ✓

Picklist for each: Bank, Employees NI, Employers NI, HM Revenue and Customs, Income Tax, Net wages, Trade union, Wages control, Wages expense.

11   DEV'S

Dev's pays its employees by cheque every month and maintains a wages control account. A summary of last month's payroll transactions is shown below:

Item	£
Gross wages	12,500
Employers' NI	1,463
Employees' NI	1,175
Income tax	3,613
Trade union fees	500

Record the journal entries needed in the general ledger to:

(i)   **Record the wages expense**

(ii)   **Record the HM Revenue and Customs liability**

(iii)   **Record the net wages paid to the employees**

(iv)   **Record the trade union liability**

(i)

Account name	Amount £	Debit ✔	Credit ✔

(ii)

Account name	Amount £	Debit ✔	Credit ✔

(iii)

Account name	Amount £	Debit ✔	Credit ✔

(iv)

Account name	Amount £	Debit ✔	Credit ✔

Picklist for each: Bank, Employees NI, Employers NI, HM Revenue and Customs, Income tax, Net wages, Pension, Trade union, Wages control, Wages expense.

IRRECOVERABLE DEBTS, CONTRAS AND TYPES OF ERROR

12 BEDROOM BITS 2

A credit customer, ABC Ltd, has ceased trading, owing Bedroom Bits £2,400 including VAT.

Record the journal entries needed in the general ledger to write off the net amount and the VAT.

Account name	Amount £	Debit ✓	Credit ✓

Picklist: Irrecoverable debts, ABC Ltd, Bedroom Bits, Purchases, Purchases ledger control, Sales, Sales ledger control, VAT.

13 GARDEN GATES 2

A credit customer, A B Landscapes Ltd, has ceased trading, owing Garden Gates £2,600 plus VAT.

Record the journal entries needed in the general ledger to write off the net amount and the VAT.

Account name	Amount £	Debit ✓	Credit ✓

Picklist: Irrecoverable debts, A B Landscapes Ltd, Garden Gates, Purchases, Purchases ledger control, Sales, Sales ledger control, VAT.

14 CHESTNUT

On 1 December, Chestnut had a balance of £46,000 on its SLCA and £31,000 on its PLCA. It also sold goods to Cook Ltd, one of its main suppliers for £4,000. Cook was owed £12,000 for goods it had sold to Chestnut.

Perform a contra and balance off the ledger accounts below. Dates are not required.

SLCA

Details	Amount £	Details	Amount £

PLCA

Details	Amount £	Details	Amount £

15   ALLEN

On 1 December, Allen had a balance of £49,000 on its PLCA and £56,000 on its SLCA. It purchased goods from Dulieu Ltd, one of its main customers, for £11,000. Dulieu owed Allen £23,000 for goods it had purchased from Allen.

Perform a contra and balance off the ledger accounts below. Dates are not required.

SLCA

Details	Amount £	Details	Amount £

PLCA

Details	Amount £	Details	Amount £

16   ERROR TYPES 1

Show which of the errors below are, or are not, disclosed by the trial balance.

Error in the general ledger	Error disclosed by the trial balance ✓	Error NOT disclosed by the trial balance ✓
Incorrectly calculating the balance on the Motor Vehicles account.		
Recording a receipt for commission received in the bank interest received account.		
Recording a bank receipt for bank interest received on the debit side of both the bank account and the bank interest received account.		
Recording supplier invoices on the debit side of the purchase ledger control account and the credit side of the purchases account		
Recording a payment by cheque to a payable in the purchase ledger control account only.		
Recording a bank payment of £124 for insurance as £142 in the insurance account and £124 in the bank account.		

17   ERROR TYPES 2

Show which of the errors below are, or are not, disclosed by the trial balance.

Error in the general ledger	Error disclosed by the trial balance ✓	Error NOT disclosed by the trial balance ✓
Recording a bank receipt for rent received on the credit side of both the bank account and rent received account.		
Recording a payment for new machinery in the equipment hire account.		
Recording a purchase return on the credit side of the purchase ledger control account and the debit side of the purchase returns account.		
Incorrectly calculating the balance on the bank interest received account.		
Recording a payment by cheque to a payable in the bank account only.		
Recording a bank payment of £120 for stationery as £210 in both accounts.		

18   ERROR TYPES 3

Match each error description with the correct type of error by placing the appropriate answer in the table below.

Error in the general ledger	Type of error
Recording a bank receipt for rent received on the credit side of both the bank account and rent received account.	
Recording a payment for new machinery in the equipment hire account.	
Recording a purchase return on the credit side of the PLCA and the debit side of the purchase returns account.	

Picklist: Transposition error, compensating error, error of original entry, error of omission, error of commission, error of principle, reversal of entries, casting error, single entry, extraction error, two entries on one side

19   ERROR TYPES 4

Match each error description with the correct type of error by placing the appropriate answer in the table below.

Error in the general ledger	Type of error
Recording a payment to a payable in the bank account only.	
Recording a bank payment of £100 for stationery as £210 in both accounts.	
Recording a receipt for commission received in the bank interest received account.	

Picklist for all above: Transposition error, compensating error, error of original entry, error of omission, error of commission, error of principle, reversal of entries, casting error, single entry, extraction error, two entries on one side

20   ERROR TYPES 5

Match each error description with the correct type of error by placing the appropriate answer in the table below.

Error in the general ledger	Type of error
A credit sale made at the month end was not recorded.	
Recording a bank payment of £120 for stationery as £210 in the stationery account and correctly in the bank account.	
Recording a receipt for commission received in the PLCA.	

Picklist for all above: Transposition error, compensating error, error of original entry, error of omission, error of commission, error of principle, reversal of entries, casting error, single entry, extraction error, two entries on one side.

21 PRINCIPLES

(a) **Show which error is an error of principle.**

Error in the general ledger	✓
Incorrectly totalling up the sales day book.	
Recording a bank payment for rent on the debit side of the office equipment account.	
Recording rent received as a debit entry in the rent and rates account.	
Recording a payment to a supplier in the purchase ledger only.	

(b) **Show which error represents two entries on one side.**

Error in the general ledger	✓
Incorrectly totalling up the sales day book.	
Recording a bank payment for rent on the debit side of the office equipment account.	
Recording rent received as a debit entry in the rent and rates account.	
Recording a payment to a supplier in the purchase ledger only.	

22 EXTRACTION

(a) **Show which error is an error of extraction.**

Error in the general ledger	✓
Incorrectly totalling up the sales day book.	
Totalling the sales day book correctly but entering the total into the SLCA as a credit balance.	
Recording drawings as a debit to drawings and a credit to cash.	
Forgetting to post the entries for payroll.	

(b) **Show which error represents an error of original entry.**

Error in the general ledger	✓
Posting a £210 invoice for electricity as £210 in the electricity account but £120 in the bank account.	
Posting an invoice for electricity as a debit in both the electricity and bank accounts.	
Posting electricity expense as a credit to electricity and a debit to the bank account.	
Posting a £200 invoice for electricity as £210 in both the electricity and bank account.	

ERRORS

23 BANK ERROR

An entry to record a bank payment of £750 for repairs has been reversed.

Record the journal entries needed in the general ledger to

(i) **remove the incorrect entry.**

(ii) **record the correct entry.**

(i)

Account name	Amount £	Debit ✓	Credit ✓

(ii)

Account name	Amount £	Debit ✓	Credit ✓

Picklist for all above: Bank, Cash, Rent, Purchases, Purchases ledger control, Repairs, Sales, Sales ledger control, Suspense, VAT.

24 RENT ERROR

An entry to record a bank receipt of £500 for rent has been reversed.

Record the journal entries needed in the general ledger to:

(i) **remove the incorrect entry.**

(ii) **record the correct entry.**

(i)

Account name	Amount £	Debit ✓	Credit ✓

(ii)

Account name	Amount £	Debit ✓	Credit ✓

Picklist for all above: Bank, Cash, Rent Received, Purchases, Purchases ledger control, Sales, Sales ledger control, Suspense, VAT.

25 GAS ERROR

An entry to record a gas expense of £300 was made correctly in the bank but was posted to electricity expenses instead of gas expenses.

Record the journal entries needed in the general ledger to record the correction.

Account name	Amount £	Debit ✓	Credit ✓

26 BUILDING ERROR

An entity purchased a new building for £400,000. This amount was debited to the buildings account, but £40,000 was credited to the bank account.

Record the journal entries needed in the general ledger to record the correction.

Account name	Amount £	Debit ✓	Credit ✓

27 SALES ERROR

A credit sale of £12,000 including VAT has been made. The full £12,000 has been debited to the SLCA and credited to sales.

Record the journal entries needed in the general ledger to record the correction.

Account name	Amount £	Debit ✓	Credit ✓

BALANCING THE TRIAL BALANCE AND CORRECTION OF ERRORS

28   CB INTERIORS

CB Interiors' initial trial balance includes a suspense account with a balance of £8,640.

The error has been traced to the purchase day-book shown below.

Purchase day-book

Date 20XX	Details	Invoice number	Total £	VAT £	Net £
30 Jun	Able Paints Ltd	2,763	2,400	400	2,000
30 Jun	Matley Materials	2,764	3,120	520	2,600
30 Jun	Teesdale Parts	2,765	4,080	680	3,400
	Totals		960	1,600	8,000

(a)   **Identify the error and record the journal entries needed in the general ledger to**

(i)   **remove the incorrect entry**

(ii)   **record the correct entry**

(iii)   **remove the suspense account balance.**

(i)

Account name	Amount £	Debit ✓	Credit ✓

(ii)

Account name	Amount £	Debit ✓	Credit ✓

(iii)

Account name	Amount £	Debit ✓	Credit ✓

Picklist for all above: Able Paints Ltd, Matley Materials, Teesdale Parts, Purchases,   Purchases day-book, Purchases ledger control, Purchases returns, Purchases returns day-book, Sales, Sales day-book, Sales ledger control, Sales returns, Sales returns day-book, Suspense, VAT.

29   ROGER DODGER

Roger Dodger's initial trial balance includes a suspense account with a balance of £360.

The error has been traced to the purchase returns day-book shown below.

Purchase returns day-book

Date 20XX	Details	Note number	Total £	VAT £	Net £
30 Jun	Dennis Designs Ltd	421	1,200	200	1,000
30 Jun	XYZ Ltd	422	1,920	320	1,600
30 Jun	Denby Prints	423	4,800	800	4,000
	Totals		7,920	1,680	6,600

(a)   **Identify the error and record the journal entries needed in the general ledger to:**

(i)   **remove the incorrect entry**

(ii)   **record the correct entry**

(iii)   **remove the suspense account balance.**

(i)

Account name	Amount £	Debit ✓	Credit ✓

(ii)

Account name	Amount £	Debit ✓	Credit ✓

(iii)

Account name	Amount £	Debit ✓	Credit ✓

Picklist for all above: Dennis Designs Ltd, XYZ Ltd, Denby Prints, Purchases, Purchases day-book, Purchases ledger control, Purchases returns, Purchases returns day-book, Sales, Sales day-book, Sales ledger control, Sales returns, Sales returns day-book, Suspense, VAT.

30 A CUT ABOVE

A Cut Above's initial trial balance includes a suspense account with a balance of £230. The error has been traced to the purchase returns day-book shown below.

Purchases returns day-book

Date 20XX	Details	Returns note number	Total £	VAT £	Net £
30 April	A & S Timber Ltd	12 – 356K	576	96	480
30 April	GB Tools	AB768 – 2	816	136	680
30 April	LAH Ltd	236	4,560	760	3,800
	Totals		6,182	992	4,960

(a) **Identify the error and record the journal entries needed in the general ledger to:**

(i) **remove the incorrect entry**

(ii) **record the correct entry**

(iii) **remove the suspense account balance.**

(i)

Account name	Amount £	Debit ✓	Credit ✓

(ii)

Account name	Amount £	Debit ✓	Credit ✓

(iii)

Account name	Amount £	Debit ✓	Credit ✓

Picklist for all above: A & S Timber Ltd, GB Tools, LAH Ltd, Purchases, Purchases day-book, Purchases ledger control, Purchases returns, Purchase returns day-books, Sales, Sales day-book, Sales ledger control, Sales returns, Sales returns day-books, Suspense, VAT.

31   RESTCO

Restco's initial trial balance includes a suspense account with a balance of £720.

The error has been traced to the sales day-book shown below.

Sales day-book

Date 20XX	Details	Invoice number	Total £	VAT £	Net £
30 Jun	Ben's Build Ltd	11232	2,160	360	1,800
30 Jun	OPP Ltd	11233	3,360	560	2,800
30 Jun	Outside Capers	11234	5,040	840	4,200
	Totals		10,560	1,760	8,080

(a)   **Identify the error and record the journal entries needed in the general ledger to**

(i)   **remove the incorrect entry**

(ii)   **record the correct entry**

(iii)   **remove the suspense account balance.**

(i)

Account name	Amount £	Debit ✓	Credit ✓

(ii)

Account name	Amount £	Debit ✓	Credit ✓

(iii)

Account name	Amount £	Debit ✓	Credit ✓

Picklist for all above: Ben's Build Ltd, OPP Ltd, Outside Capers, Purchases, Purchases day-book, Purchases ledger control, Purchases returns, Purchases returns day-book, Sales, Sales day-book, Sales ledger control, Sales returns, Sales returns day-book, Suspense, VAT.

32   JOHNNY JOINER

Johnny Joiner's trial balance was extracted and did not balance. The debit column of the trial balance totalled £442,735 and the credit column totalled £428,372.

(a)   **What entry would be made in the suspense account to balance the trial balance.**

Account name	Amount £	Debit ✓	Credit ✓
Suspense			

(b)   The error has been traced to sales, which were posted as £241,874 instead of £256,237.

Record the journal entries needed in the general ledger to record the correction.

Account name	Amount £	Debit ✓	Credit ✓

33   BUCKLEY DRAINS

Buckley Drains' trial balance was extracted and did not balance. The debit column of the trial balance totalled £336,728 and the credit column totalled £325,923.

(a)   **What entry would be made in the suspense account to balance the trial balance.**

Account name	Amount £	Debit ✓	Credit ✓
Suspense			

(b)   The error has been traced to an unpaid invoice for advertising, which was recorded correctly in advertising expenses but nowhere else.

Record the journal entries needed in the general ledger to record the correction.

Account name	Amount £	Debit ✓	Credit ✓

(c)   **Show one reason for maintaining the journal**

	✓
To correct errors only	
To correct errors and record transactions that have not been recorded in any other book of prime entry	
To record transactions from every other book of prime entry.	

34 MENDONCA

Mendonca's trial balance was extracted and did not balance. The debit column of the trial balance totalled £643,475 and the credit column totalled £641,495

(a) **What entry would be made in the suspense account to balance the trial balance?**

Account name	Amount £	Debit ✓	Credit ✓

(b) The error has been traced to the posting of the wages payment. The total payment made was £3,200. This was incorrectly made in both the wages and bank account. The amount recorded in wages was £2,300, with a credit to the bank of £320 shown. **Record the journal entries needed in the general ledger to record the correction.**

Account name	Amount £	Debit ✓	Credit ✓

35 BEASANT

Beasant's trial balance was extracted and did not balance. The debit column of the trial balance totalled £630,000 and the credit column totalled £615,000.

(a) **What entry would be made in the suspense account to balance the trial balance.**

Account name	Amount £	Debit ✓	Credit ✓
Suspense			

(b) The error has been traced to a late credit sale. The full amount of the sale (including VAT) was correctly recorded in the SLCA but no other entries were made. **Record the journal entries needed in the general ledger to record the correction.**

Account name	Amount £	Debit ✓	Credit ✓

(c) **Show one reason for maintaining the journal**

	✓
To detect fraud	
To record non-regular transactions	
To record goods sold on credit	

POSTING JOURNAL ENTRIES TO LEDGER ACCOUNTS

36 PAT'S CAFE

Pat's Cafe's trial balance included a suspense account. All the bookkeeping errors have now been traced and the journal entries shown below have been recorded.

Journal entries

Account name	Debit £	Credit £
Bank interest paid	114	
Bank interest received		114
Insurance	150	
Suspense		150
Suspense	4,500	
Motor vehicles		4,500

Post the journal entries to the general ledger accounts. Dates are not required.

Bank interest paid

Details	Amount £	Details	Amount £

Bank interest received

Details	Amount £	Details	Amount £

Suspense

Details	Amount £	Details	Amount £
		Balance b/d	4,350

Insurance

Details	Amount £	Details	Amount £

Motor vehicles

Details	Amount £	Details	Amount £

Picklists: Balance b/d, Bank Interest Paid, Bank Interest Received, Insurance, Motor Vehicles, Suspense.

37 TWINKLE'S TRINKETS

Twinkle's Trinkets trial balance included a suspense account. All the bookkeeping errors have now been traced and the journal entries shown below have been recorded.

Journal entries

Account name	Debit £	Credit £
Motor expenses	324	
Suspense		324
Suspense	1,100	
Repairs and renewals		1,100
Rent payable	500	
Rent received		500

Post the journal entries to the general ledger accounts. Dates are not required.

Motor expenses

Details	Amount £	Details	Amount £

Repairs and renewals

Details	Amount £	Details	Amount £

Suspense

Details	Amount £	Details	Amount £
		Balance b/d	776

Rent received

Details	Amount £	Details	Amount £

Rent payable

Details	Amount £	Details	Amount £

Picklists: Balance b/d, Rent payable, Rent received, Motor expenses, Repairs and renewals, Suspense.

38   SPARKS AND MENCER

Sparks and Mencer's trial balance included a suspense account. All the bookkeeping errors have now been traced and the journal entries shown below have been recorded.

Journal entries

Account name	Debit £	Credit £
Heat and light		545
Suspense	545	
Rates	786	
Suspense		786
Loan interest expense	269	
Bank interest received		269

Post the journal entries to the general ledger accounts. Dates are not required.

Heat and light

Details	Amount £	Details	Amount £

Rates

Details	Amount £	Details	Amount £

Suspense

Details	Amount £	Details	Amount £
Balance b/d	241		

Loan interest expense

Details	Amount £	Details	Amount £

Bank interest received

Details	Amount £	Details	Amount £

Picklist: Balance b/d, Bank interest received, Loan interest expense, Bank interest paid, Heat and light, Rates, Suspense.

39 PIRATE PETE'S

Pirate Pete's trial balance included a suspense account. All the bookkeeping errors have now been traced and the journal entries shown below have been recorded.

Journal entries

Account name	Debit £	Credit £
Commission paid	450	
Commission received		450
Light and heat	489	
Suspense		489
Suspense	2,424	
Plant and machinery		2,424

Post the journal entries to the general ledger accounts. Dates are not required.

Commission paid

Details	Amount £	Details	Amount £

Commission received

Details	Amount £	Details	Amount £

Suspense

Details	Amount £	Details	Amount £
		Balance b/d	1,935

Light and heat

Details	Amount £	Details	Amount £

Plant and machinery

Details	Amount £	Details	Amount £

Picklists: Balance b/d, Commission Paid, Commission received, Light and heat, Plant and machinery, Suspense.

RE-DRAFT THE TRIAL BALANCE

40   RICK'S RACERS

On 30 June Rick's Racers extracted an initial trial balance which did not balance, and a suspense account was opened. On 1 July journal entries were prepared to correct the errors that had been found, and clear the suspense account. The list of balances in the initial trial balance, and the journal entries to correct the errors, are shown below.

Re-draft the trial balance by placing the figures in the debit or credit column. You should take into account the journal entries which will clear the suspense account.

	Balances extracted on 30 June £	Balances at 1 July	
		Debit £	Credit £
Motor vehicles	24,200		
Plant and equipment	22,350		
Inventory	9,000		
Cash at bank	11,217		
Cash	150		
Sales ledger control	131,275		
Purchases ledger control	75,336		
VAT owing to HM Revenue and Customs	15,127		
Capital	14,417		
Bank loan	12,500		
Sales	276,132		
Purchases	152,476		
Wages	35,465		
Motor expenses	3,617		
Repairs and renewals	2,103		
Rent and rates	3,283		
Light and heat	4,012		
Insurance	4,874		
Sundry expenses	1,230		
Suspense account (credit balance)	11,740		
Totals			

Journal entries

Account name	Debit £	Credit £
Capital		9,500
Suspense	9,500	
Capital		2,330
Suspense	2,330	

Account name	Debit £	Credit £
Suspense	1,230	
Sundry expenses		1,230
Sundry expenses	1,320	
Suspense		1,320

41 PERCY POTS

On 30 June Percy Pots extracted an initial trial balance which did not balance, and a suspense account was opened. On 1 July journal entries were prepared to correct the errors that had been found, and clear the suspense account. The list of balances in the initial trial balance, and the journal entries to correct the errors, are shown below.

Re-draft the trial balance by placing the figures in the debit or credit column. You should take into account the journal entries which will clear the suspense account.

	Balances extracted on 30 June £	Balances at 1 July	
		Debit £	Credit £
Motor vehicles	22,348		
Fixtures and fittings	9,234		
Inventory	4,800		
Bank	2,661		
Petty cash	100		
Sales ledger control	61,025		
Purchases ledger control	35,275		
VAT owing to HM Revenue and Customs	4,630		
Capital	4,852		
Sales	142,378		
Sales returns	1,780		
Purchases	69,276		

Wages	13,500		
Motor expenses	873		
Office expenses	1,796		
Rent and rates	1,276		
Heat and light	1,022		
Insurance	1,629		
Miscellaneous expenses	1,047		
Suspense account (credit balance)	5,232		
Totals			

Journal entries

Account name	Debit £	Credit £
Bank		2,661
Suspense	2,661	
Bank		2,661
Suspense	2,661	

Account name	Debit £	Credit £
Sales returns	1,870	
Suspense		1,870
Sales returns		1,780
Suspense	1,780	

42   IVOR ISLAND

On 30 April Ivor Island extracted an initial trial balance which did not balance, and a suspense account was opened. On 1 May journal entries were prepared to correct the errors that had been found, and clear the suspense account. The list of balances in the initial trial balance, and the journal entries to correct the errors, are shown below.

Redraft the trial balance by placing the figures in the debit or credit column. You should take into account the journal entries below which will clear the suspense account.

	Balances extracted on 30 April	Balances at 1 May	
		Debit £	Credit £
Motor vehicles	8,454		
Office building	28,676		
Inventory	15,369		
Bank	26,984		
Petty cash	459		
Sales ledger control	35,987		
Purchases ledger control	26,942		
VAT (owing from HM Revenue and Customs)	231		
Capital	98,106		
Sales	96,325		
Sales returns (credit balance)	3,654		
Purchases	68,975		
Wages	18,564		
Motor expenses	1,269		
Office expenses	5,798		
Rates	4,300		
Heat and light	5,423		
Insurance	3,365		
Misc expenses	2,645		
Suspense account (credit balance)	1,472		

Journal entries:

Account name	Debit £	Credit £
VAT		586
Suspense	586	
VAT		586
Suspense	586	

Account name	Debit £	Credit £
Sales returns		2,556
Suspense	2,556	
Sales returns	2,256	
Suspense		2,256

43   RING OF ROSES

On 30 June Ring of Roses extracted an initial trial balance which did not balance, and a suspense account was opened. On 1 July journal entries were prepared to correct the errors that had been found, and clear the suspense account. The list of balances in the initial trial balance, and the journal entries to correct the errors, are shown below.

Re-draft the trial balance by placing the figures in the debit or credit column. You should take into account the journal entries which will clear the suspense account.

	Balances extracted on 30 June £	Balances at 1 July	
		Debit £	Credit £
Motor vehicles	27,625		
Plant and equipment	5,000		
Inventory	7,350		
Cash at bank	7,195		
Cash	200		
Sales ledger control	121,275		
Purchases ledger control	67,323		
VAT owing to HM Revenue and Customs	10,098		
Capital	22,291		
Sales	253,727		
Sales returns	2,123		
Purchases	128,476		
Purchase returns	9,872		
Wages	34,250		
Motor expenses	1,797		
Office expenses	4,946		
Rent and rates	2,321		
Heat and light	3,123		
Insurance	4,205		
Suspense account (debit balance)	13,425		
Totals			

Journal entries

Account name	Debit £	Credit £
Bank	7,150	
Suspense		7,150
Purchases	6,455	
Suspense		6,455

Account name	Debit £	Credit £
Suspense	4,205	
Insurance		4,205
Insurance	4,025	
Suspense		4,025

44   HEARN

On 30 June Hearn extracted an initial trial balance which did not balance, and a suspense account was opened. On 1 July the following errors were noted:

1   A rent payment of £430 had been correctly included in the bank, but included within rent expenses as £340.

2   An irrecoverable debt of £600 plus VAT had been credited correctly credited to the SLCA, but the only debit entry was £600 to irrecoverable debts.

Complete the journal to correct the errors, and re-draft the trial balance by placing figures into the debit or credit column. You re-drafted trial balance should take into account the journal entries you have made.

Journal entries

Account name	Debit £	Credit £

	Balances extracted on 30 June £	Balances at 1 July	
		Debit £	Credit £
Sales ledger control	34,560		
Purchases ledger control	21,420		
VAT owing to HM Revenue and Customs	3,412		
Capital	50,000		
Sales	201,327		
Sales returns	1,465		
Purchases	87,521		
Purchase returns	252		
Plant and equipment	15,200		
Motor expenses	4,310		
Office expenses	10,321		
Rent and rates	21,420		
Heat and light	8,920		
Wages	53,205		
Irrecoverable debt	1,450		
Office equipment	42,030		
Bank overdraft	4201		
Suspense account (debit balance)	210		
Totals			

45 RODMAN

On 30 June Rodman extracted an initial trial balance which did not balance, and a suspense account was opened. On 1 July the following errors were noted:

1   A VAT refund of £1,250 received from HMRC was recorded in the bank, but no other entry was made.

2   A wages payment of £4,300 was credited to both the bank and wages.

Complete the journal to correct the errors, and re-draft the trial balance by placing figures into the debit or credit column. You re-drafted trial balance should take into account the journal entries you have made.

Journal entries

Account name	Debit £	Credit £

	Balances extracted on 30 June £	Balances at 1 July	
		Debit £	Credit £
Sales ledger control	38,070		
Purchases ledger control	20,310		
VAT owed from HM Revenue and Customs	2,510		
Capital	70,000		
Sales	153,488		
Sales returns	2,135		
Purchases	63,261		
Purchase returns	542		
Plant and equipment	17,319		
Motor expenses	3,214		
Office expenses	6,421		
Rent and rates	17,414		
Heat and light	6,421		
Wages	45,532		
Irrecoverable debt	1,532		
Office equipment	35,313		
Bank overdraft	2,152		
Suspense account (debit balance)	7,350		
Totals			

UPDATE THE CASH BOOK

46   RIVERS LTD

The bank statement and cash book of Rivers is shown below.

Midway Bank PLC 52 The Parade, Middleton, MD1 9LA				
To: Rivers Ltd	Account No: 28012877		23 June 20XX	
Statement of Account				
Date	**Detail**	**Paid out**	**Paid in**	**Balance**
20XX		£	£	£
04 June	Balance b/d			3,115 C
04 June	Cheque 101013	650		2,465 C
04 June	Cheque 101014	1,420		1,045 C
05 June	Cheque 101015	60		985 C
07 June	Cheque 101018	450		535 C
12 June	Bank Giro credit Ayreshire build		970	1,505 C
13 June	Cheque 101016	615		890 C
15 June	Direct debit COLLINS	175		715 C
19 June	Paid in at Midway bank		300	1,015 C
20 June	Direct debit rent	500		515 C
23 June	Bank interest		15	530 C
23 June	Bank charges	20		510 C
D = Debit C = Credit				

Date 20XX	Details	Bank £	Date 20XX	Cheque number	Details	Bank £
01 June	Balance b/d	3,115	01 June	101013	Indigo Beds	650
17 June	Bracken Ltd	300	01 June	101014	DirectFit	1,420
21 June	Airfleet Interiors	560	01 June	101015	Langdon	60
22 June	Harris Homes	333	02 June	101016	QPF Ltd	615
			03 June	101017	OMD Ltd	815
			03 June	101018	Hamden Ltd	450
			15 June	101019	Freeman and Cope	522
			15 June		COLLINS	175

Details columns options: Balance b/d, Balance c/d, Bank charges, QPF Ltd, Bracken Ltd, Ayrshire build, Closing balance, Directfit, Hamden Ltd, Rent, COLLINS, Langdon, Airfleet Interiors, Freeman and Cope, OMD Ltd, Opening balance, Bank Interest, Indigo Beds, Harris Homes.

(a)   **Check the items on the bank statement against the items in the cash book.**

(b)   **Enter any items in the cash book as needed.**

(c)   **Total the cash book and clearly show the balance carried down at 23 June (closing balance) and brought down at 24 June (opening balance).**

47   LUXURY BATHROOMS

On 28 April Luxury Bathrooms received the following bank statement as at 24 April.

SKB Bank plc				
68 London Road, Reading, RG8 4RN				
To: Luxury Bathrooms	Account No: 55548921		24 April 20XX	
Statement of Account				
Date	**Detail**	**Paid out**	**Paid in**	**Balance**
20XX		£	£	£
03 April	Balance b/d			17,845 C
03 April	Cheque 120045	8,850		8,995 C
04 April	Bank Giro Ricketts & Co		465	9,460 C
04 April	Cheque 120046	2,250		7,210 C
05 April	Cheque 120047	64		7,146 C
08 April	Cheque 120048	3,256		3,890 C
14 April	Direct debit AMB Ltd	2,265		1,625 C
14 April	Direct debit D Draper	2,950		1,325 D
14 April	Cheque 120050	655		1,980 D
22 April	Paid in at SKB bank		2,150	170 C
22 April	Bank charges	63		107 C
23 April	Overdraft fee	25		82 C
D = Debit C = Credit				

The cash book as at 24 April is shown below.

Cash book

Date	Details	Bank	Date	Cheque	Details	Bank
01 April	Balance b/d	17,845	01 April	120045	R Sterling Ltd	8,850
19 April	Olsen & Lane	2,150	01 April	120046	Bert Cooper	2,250
22 April	Frith Ltd	685	01 April	120047	Hetko & Sons	64
22 April	Hodgetts & Co	282	02 April	120048	Barrett Ltd	3,256
			02 April	120049	K Plomer	542
			08 April	120050	I&E Brown	655
			08 April	120051	T Roberts	1,698
			14 April		AMB Ltd	2,265

Details column options: Balance b/d, balance c/d, Bank charges, R Sterling Ltd, Olsen & Lane, Frith Ltd, Hodgetts & Co, Bert Cooper, Hetko & Sons, Barrett Ltd, K Plomer, I&E Brown, T Roberts, AMB Ltd, Ricketts & Co, D Draper, Opening balance, Overdraft fees.

(a) **Check the items on the bank statement against the items in the cash book.**

(b) **Enter any items in the cash book as needed.**

(c) **Total the cash book and clearly show the balance carried down at 24 April (closing balance) and brought down at 25 April (opening balance).**

48   WHOLESALE FLOORING

The bank statement and cash book for Wholesale Flooring is shown below.

Money Bags Bank PLC
52 Oak Road, Timperley, SK10 8LR

To: Wholesale Flooring   Account No: 47013799   23 June 20XX

Statement of Account

Date 20XX	Detail	Paid out £	Paid in £	Balance £	
04 June	Balance b/d			5,125	D
05 June	Cheque 104373	890		6,015	D
05 June	Cheque 104374	1,725		7,740	D
05 June	Cheque 104375	210		7,950	D
11 June	Cheque 104378	784		8,734	D
12 June	Bank Giro credit Aintree and Co		1,250	7,484	D
13 June	Cheque 104376	1,275		8,759	D
15 June	Cheque 104377	725		9,484	D
17 June	Paid in at Money Bags bank plc		550	8,934	D
20 June	Direct debit MD County council	400		9,334	D
23 June	Bank charges	160		9,494	D
23 June	Overdraft fee	90		9,584	D

D = Debit   C = Credit

Cash book

Date 20XX	Details	Bank £	Date 20XX	Cheque number	Details	Bank £
			01 June		Balance b/d	5,125
16 June	Beeston's	550	01 June	104373	Good iron	890
19 June	Airfleet exteriors	3,025	01 June	104374	Ashworth & Co	1,725
22 June	Jones's	2,775	01 June	104375	Ironfit	210
			05 June	104376	OSS Ltd	1,275
			07 June	104377	Perfect tools	725
			08 June	104378	Campden Ltd	784
			14 June	104379	Thornley & Thwaite	675
			14 June	104380	Castle & Cove	178

Details columns options: Balance b/d, Balance c/d, Bank charges, Good Iron, Beeston's, Aintree & Co, Perfect Tools, Closing balance, Ashworth & Co, Thornley & Thwaite, MD County Council, Campden Ltd, Airfleet Exteriors, Castle & Cove, OSS Ltd, Opening balance, Overdraft Fee, Ironfit, Jones's.

(a)   **Check the items on the bank statement against the items in the cash book.**

(b)   **Enter any items in the cash book as needed.**

(c)   **Total the cash book and clearly show the balance carried down at 23 June (closing balance) and brought down at 24 June (opening balance).**

49   24 HOUR TAXIS

On 28 June 24 Hour Taxis received the following bank statement as at 23 June.

Four Kings Bank PLC
124 Four Kings Way, Newton Mearns, GL10 5QR

| To: 24 Hour Taxis | Account No: 16135844 | | 23 June 20XX | |

Statement of Account

Date 20XX	Detail	Paid out £	Paid in £	Balance £	
04 June	Balance b/d			6,025	C
05 June	Cheque 102597	910		5,115	C
05 June	Cheque 102598	2,010		3,105	C
05 June	Cheque 102599	315		2,790	C
11 June	Cheque 102602	675		2,115	C
12 June	Bank Giro credit Barron Homes		1,475	3,590	C
13 June	Cheque 102600	1,725		1,865	C
15 June	Cheque 102601	686		1,179	C
17 June	Paid in at Four Kings Bank		1,000	2,179	C
20 June	Direct debit AB Insurance	1,250		929	C
23 June	Bank charges	50		879	C
23 June	Overdraft fee	25		854	C
	D = Debit C = Credit				

Cash book

Date 20XX	Details	Bank £	Date 20XX	Cheque number	Details	Bank £
01 June	Balance b/d	6,025	01 June	102597	Best ideas	910
18 June	Earnshaw's	1,000	02 June	102598	Bentley & Burn	2,010
19 June	Mainstreet Ltd	1,206	02 June	102599	Bits & Bats	315
21 June	Housley Inc	1,725	03 June	102600	LPF Ltd	1,725
			07 June	102601	Essentials	686
			08 June	102602	Hopburn Ltd	675
			15 June	102603	Thistle Tools	410
			15 June	102604	C Campbell Ltd	275

Details columns options: Balance b/d, Balance c/d, Bank charges, Earnshaw's, Housley Inc, C Campbell Ltd, Mainstreet Ltd, Closing balance, Barron Homes, Thistle Tools, AB Insurance, Hopburn Ltd, Best Ideas, Bentley & Burn, LPF Ltd, Opening balance, Overdraft Fee, Bits & Bats, Essentials.

(a)   **Check the items on the bank statement against the items in the cash book.**

(b)   **Enter any items in the cash book as needed.**

(c)   **Total the cash book and clearly show the balance carried down at 23 June (closing balance) and brought down at 24 June (opening balance).**

50   WOOD

The bank statement and cash book for Wood is shown below.

Money Bags Bank PLC				
52 Oak Road, Timperley, SK10 8LR				
To: Wood Ltd	Account No: 47013799		23 June 20XX	

Statement of Account

Date	Detail	Paid out	Paid in	Balance	
20XX		£	£	£	
04 June	Balance b/d			17,640	C
05 June	Bank Giro credit Bradley		1,320	18,960	C
05 June	Bank Giro credit Thanoj		2,450	21,410	C
05 June	Paid in at Money Bags bank PLC		9,420	30,830	C
11 June	Cheque 110341	1,540		29,290	C
12 June	BACS payment Southwell	820		28,470	C
13 June	Cheque 110343	750		27,720	C
15 June	Cheque 110344	570		27,150	C
17 June	Interest earned		80	27,230	C
20 June	Direct debit Blundell	400		26,830	C
23 June	BACS payment Bore	250		26,580	C
23 June	Cheque 110346	740		25,840	C
D = Debit C = Credit					

Cash book

Date 20XX	Details	Bank £	Date 20XX	Cheque number	Details	Bank £
01 June	Balance b/d	17,640				
03 June	Bradley	1,320	04 June	110341	Carr	1,540
03 June	Cash sales	9,420	04 June	110342	Ramsden	980
03 June	Thanoj	2,450	04 June	110343	Coulson	750
21 June	Cash sales	7,430	04 June	110344	Brodie	570
21 June	Devitt	1,990	04 June	110345	Jones	550
			04 June	110346	Gritton	740
			20 June		Bore	250

(a)   **Check the items on the bank statement against the items in the cash book.**

(b)   **Enter any items in the cash book as needed.**

(c)   **Total the cash book and clearly show the balance carried down at 23 June (closing balance) and brought down at 24 June (opening balance).**

51 PEARSON

The bank statement and cash book for Pearson is shown below:

Money Bags Bank PLC

To: Pearson Ltd   Account No: 47013799   23 June 20XX

Statement of Account

Date 20XX	Detail	Paid out £	Paid in £	Balance £	
01 June	Balance b/d			1,340	D
02 June	Bank Giro credit Pond		1,890	550	C
02 June	Interest received		5	555	C
02 June	Direct Debit McMenemy	1,200		645	D
11 June	Cheque 110123	430		1,075	D
12 June	Paid in to Money Bags bank		840	235	D
13 June	Cheque 110126	75		310	D
15 June	Cheque 110127	270		580	D
17 June	Paid in to Money Bags bank		1,540	960	C
20 June	Direct debit Findus	300		660	C
23 June	Bank charges	25		635	C
23 June	Cheque 110129	740		105	D
	D = Debit C = Credit				

Cash book

Date 20XX	Details	Bank £	Date 20XX	Cheque number	Details	Bank £
01 June	Balance b/d	550	07 June	110123	Connell	430
09 June	Cash sales	840	07 June	110124	Renner	720
14 June	Cash sales	1,540	07 June	110125	Bond	750
22 June	Cunnington	1,730	07 June	110126	Hatton	75
			07 June	110127	Bull	270
			07 June	110128	Black	135
			07 June	110129	Southall	740

(a)   **Check the items on the bank statement against the items in the cash book.**

(b)   **Enter any items in the cash book as needed.**

(c)   **Total the cash book and clearly show the balance carried down at 23 June (closing balance) and brought down at 24 June (opening balance).**

52 MCKEOWN

The bank statement and cash book for McKeown is shown below.

Money Bags Bank PLC

To: McKeown Ltd   Account No: 47013799   23 June 20XX

Statement of Account

Date 20XX	Detail	Paid out £	Paid in £	Balance £	
01 June	Balance b/d			7,420	C
01 June	Bank Giro credit Pond		180	7,600	C
01 June	Cheque 110156	420		7,180	C
01 June	Interest received		85	7,265	C
11 June	Cheque 110157	430		6,835	C
12 June	Cheque 110158	520		6,315	C
13 June	Cheque 110161	750		5,565	C
15 June	Bank Giro credit Sherwood		640	6,205	C
17 June	Paid in to Money Bags bank		1,200	7,405	C
20 June	Bank Giro credit Coyne		1,630	9,035	C
23 June	Direct debit Wilmott	300		8,735	C
23 June	Interest received		35	8,770	C

D = Debit   C = Credit

Cash book

Date 20XX	Details	Bank £	Date 20XX	Cheque number	Details	Bank £
01 June	Balance b/d	7,180	07 June	110157	Williams	430
12 June	Sherwood	640	07 June	110158	Forecast	520
14 June	Cash sales	1,200	07 June	110159	Beasant	1,240
22 June	Tweedy	860	07 June	110160	Davison	1,420
23 June	Butterwood	440	07 June	110161	Mildenhall	750

(a) **Check the items on the bank statement against the items in the cash book.**

(b) **Enter any items in the cash book as needed.**

(c) **Total the cash book and clearly show the balance carried down at 23 June (closing balance) and brought down at 24 June (opening balance).**

BANK RECONCILIATIONS

53 RIVERS BANK RECONCILIATION

Below is the bank statement and **updated** cash book for Rivers.

	Midway Bank PLC 52 The Parade, Middleton, MD1 9LA			
To: Rivers Ltd	Account No: 28012877		23 June 20XX	

Statement of Account

Date 20XX	Detail	Paid out £	Paid in £	Balance £	
04 June	Balance b/d			3,115	C
04 June	Cheque 101013	650		2,465	C
04 June	Cheque 101014	1,420		1,045	C
05 June	Cheque 101015	60		985	C
07 June	Cheque 101018	450		535	C
12 June	Bank Giro credit Ayreshire build		970	1,505	C
13 June	Cheque 101016	615		890	C
15 June	Direct debit COLLINS	175		715	C
17 June	Paid in at Midway bank		300	1,015	C
20 June	Direct debit rent	500		515	C
23 June	Bank interest		15	530	C
23 June	Bank charges	20		510	C
	D = Debit C = Credit				

Date 20XX	Details	Bank £	Date 20XX	Cheque number	Details	Bank £
01 June	Balance b/d	3,115	01 June	101013	Indigo beds	650
17 June	Bracken Ltd	300	01 June	101014	DirectFit	1,420
21 June	Airfleet Interiors	560	01 June	101015	Langdon	60
22 June	Harris Homes	333	01 June	101016	QPF Ltd	615
12 June	Ayreshire Build	970	02 June	101017	OMD Ltd	815
23 June	Bank Interest	15	02 June	101018	Hamden Ltd	450
			13 June	101019	Freeman & Cope	522
			13 June		COLLINS	175
			20 June		Rent	500
			23 June		Bank charges	20
			23 June		Balance c/d	66
		5,293				5,293
24 June	Balance b/d	66				

Complete the bank reconciliation statement as at 23 June.

Note: Do not make any entries in the shaded boxes.

Bank reconciliation statement as at 23 June 20XX

Balance per bank statement	£
Add:	
Name:	£
Name:	£
Total to add	£
Less:	
Name:	£
Name:	£
Total to subtract	£
Balance as per cash book	£

Name options: Bank charges, QPF Ltd, Bracken Ltd, Ayreshire build, Directfit, Hamden Ltd, Rent, COLLINS, Langdon, Airfleet interiors, Freeman and Cope, OMD Ltd, Bank interest, Indigo beds, Harris homes.

54 LUXURY BATHROOMS RECONCILIATION

Below is the bank statement and updated cash book for Luxury Bathrooms.

<table>
<tr><td colspan="5" align="center">SKB Bank plc</td></tr>
<tr><td colspan="5" align="center">68 London Road, Reading, RG8 4RN</td></tr>
<tr><td colspan="2">To: Luxury Bathrooms</td><td colspan="2" align="center">Account No: 55548921</td><td>24 April 20XX</td></tr>
<tr><td colspan="5" align="center">Statement of Account</td></tr>
<tr><td>Date</td><td>Detail</td><td>Paid out</td><td>Paid in</td><td>Balance</td></tr>
<tr><td>20XX</td><td></td><td>£</td><td>£</td><td>£</td></tr>
<tr><td>03 April</td><td>Balance b/d</td><td></td><td></td><td>17,845 C</td></tr>
<tr><td>03 April</td><td>Cheque 120045</td><td>8,850</td><td></td><td>8,995 C</td></tr>
<tr><td>04 April</td><td>Bank Giro Ricketts & Co</td><td></td><td>465</td><td>9,460 C</td></tr>
<tr><td>04 April</td><td>Cheque 120046</td><td>2,250</td><td></td><td>7,210 C</td></tr>
<tr><td>05 April</td><td>Cheque 120047</td><td>64</td><td></td><td>7,146 C</td></tr>
<tr><td>08 April</td><td>Cheque 120048</td><td>3,256</td><td></td><td>3,890 C</td></tr>
<tr><td>14 April</td><td>Direct debit AMB Ltd</td><td>2,265</td><td></td><td>1,625 C</td></tr>
<tr><td>14 April</td><td>Direct debit D Draper</td><td>2,950</td><td></td><td>1,325 D</td></tr>
<tr><td>14 April</td><td>Cheque 120050</td><td>655</td><td></td><td>1,980 D</td></tr>
<tr><td>22 April</td><td>Paid in at SKB Bank</td><td></td><td>2,150</td><td>170 C</td></tr>
<tr><td>22 April</td><td>Bank charges</td><td>63</td><td></td><td>107 C</td></tr>
<tr><td>23 April</td><td>Overdraft fee</td><td>25</td><td></td><td>82 C</td></tr>
<tr><td colspan="5" align="center">D = Debit   C = Credit</td></tr>
</table>

Date	Details	Bank	Date	Cheque	Details	Bank
01 April	Balance b/d	17,845	01 April	120045	R Sterling Ltd	8,850
19 April	Olsen & Lane	2,150	01 April	120046	Bert Cooper	2,250
22 April	Frith Ltd	685	01 April	120047	Hetko & Sons	64
22 April	Hodgetts & Co	282	02 April	120048	Barrett Ltd	3,256
04 April	Ricketts & Co	465	02 April	120049	K Plomer	542
			08 April	120050	I&E Brown	655
			08 April	120051	T Roberts	1,698
			14 April		AMB Ltd	2,265
			14 April		D Draper	2,950
			22 April		Bank charges	63
			23 April		Overdraft fee	25
24 April	Balance c/d	1,191				
		22,618				22,618
			25 April		Balance b/d	1,191

Complete the bank reconciliation statement as at 24 April.

Note: Do not make any entries in the shaded boxes.

Bank reconciliation statement as at 24 April 20XX.

Balance per bank statement	£
Add:	
Name:	£
Name:	£
Total to add	£
Less:	
Name:	£
Name:	£
Total to subtract	£
Balance as per cash book	£

Name options: Bank charges, , R Sterling Ltd, Olsen & Lane, Frith Ltd, Hodgetts & Co, Bert Cooper, Hetko & Sons, Barrett Ltd, K Plomer, I&E Brown, T Roberts, AMB Ltd, Ricketts & Co, D Draper, Overdraft fees.

55   WHOLESALE FLOORING BANK RECONCILIATION

Below is the bank statement and updated cash book for Wholesale Flooring.

Money Bags Bank PLC
52 Oak Road, Timperley, SK10 8LR

To: Wholesale Flooring		Account No: 47013799		23 June 20XX	
		Statement of Account			
Date	**Detail**	**Paid out**	**Paid in**	**Balance**	
20XX		£	£	£	
04 June	Balance b/d			5,125	D
05 June	Cheque 104373	890		6,015	D
05 June	Cheque 104374	1,725		7,740	D
05 June	Cheque 104375	210		7,950	D
11 June	Cheque 104378	784		8,734	D
12 June	Bank Giro credit Aintree and Co		1,250	7,484	D
13 June	Cheque 104376	1,275		8,759	D
15 June	Cheque 104377	725		9,484	D
17 June	Paid in at Money Bags bank plc		550	8,934	D
20 June	Direct debit MD County council	400		9,334	D
23 June	Bank charges	160		9,494	D
23 June	Overdraft fee	90		9,584	D
		D = Debit C = Credit			

Date 20XX	Details	Bank £	Date 20XX	Cheque number	Details	Bank £
			01 June		Balance b/d	5,125
16 June	Beeston's	550	01 June	104373	Good Iron	890
19 June	Airfleet exteriors	3,025	01 June	104374	Ashworth & Co	1,725
22 June	Jones's	2,775	01 June	104375	Ironfit	210
12 June	Aintree & Co	1,250	05 June	104376	OSS Ltd	1,275
			07 June	104377	Perfect Tools	725
			08 June	104378	Campden Ltd	784
			14 June	104379	Thornley & Thwaite	675
			14 June	104380	Castle and Cove	178
			20 June		MD County council	400
			23 June		Bank charges	160
23 June	Balance c/d	4,637	23 June		Overdraft fee	90
		12,237				12,237
			24 June		Balance b/d	4,637

Complete the bank reconciliation statement as at 23 June.

Note: Do not make any entries in the shaded boxes.

Bank reconciliation statement as at 23 June 20XX

Balance per bank statement	£
Add:	
Name:	£
Name:	£
Total to add	£
Less:	
Name:	£
Name:	£
Total to subtract	£
Balance as per cash book	£

Name options: Bank charges, OSS Ltd, Beeston's, Aintree and Co, Ironfit, Campden Ltd, MD County Council, Ashworth & Co, Airfleet Exteriors, Thornley & Thwaite, Perfect Tools, Overdraft Fee, Castle & Cove, Good Iron, Jones's.

56 24 HOUR TAXIS BANK RECONCILIATION

Below is the bank statement and updated cash book for 24 Hour Taxis.

Four Kings Bank PLC
124 Four Kings Way, Newton Mearns, GL10 5QR

To: 24 Hour Taxis   Account No: 16135844   23 June 20XX

Statement of Account

Date 20XX	Detail	Paid out £	Paid in £	Balance £	
04 June	Balance b/d			6,025	C
05 June	Cheque 102597	910		5,115	C
05 June	Cheque 102598	2,010		3,105	C
05 June	Cheque 102599	315		2,790	C
11 June	Cheque 102602	675		2,115	C
12 June	Bank Giro credit Barron Homes		1,475	3,590	C
13 June	Cheque 102600	1,725		1,865	C
15 June	Cheque 102601	686		1,179	C
18 June	Paid in at Four Kings bank		1,000	2,179	C
20 June	Direct debit AB Insurance	1,250		929	C
23 June	Bank charges	50		879	C
23 June	Overdraft fee	25		854	C
	D = Debit C = Credit				

Date 20XX	Details	Bank £	Date 20XX	Cheque number	Details	Bank £
01 June	Balance b/d	6,025	01 June	102597	Best ideas	910
18 June	Earnshaw's	1,000	02 June	102598	Bentley and Burn	2,010
19 June	Mainstreet Ltd	1,206	02 June	102599	Bits and Bats	315
21 June	Housley Inc	1,725	03 June	102600	LPF Ltd	1,725
12 June	Barron Homes	1,475	07 June	102601	Essentials	686
			08 June	102602	Hopburn Ltd	675
			15 June	102603	Thistle tools	410
			15 June	102604	C Campbell Ltd	275
			20 June		AB Insurance	1,250
			23 June		Bank charges	50
			23 June		Overdraft fee	25
			23 June		Balance c/d	3,100
		11,431				11,431
24 June	Balance b/d	3,100				

Complete the bank reconciliation statement as at 23 June.

Note: Do not make any entries in the shaded boxes.

Bank reconciliation statement as at 23 June 20XX

Balance per bank statement	£
Add:	
Name:	£
Name:	£
Total to add	£
Less:	
Name:	£
Name:	£
Total to subtract	£
Balance as per cash book	£

Name options: Bank charges, LPF Ltd, Earnshaw's, Barron Homes, Best Ideas, C Campbell Ltd, AB Insurance, Housley Inc, Mainstreet Ltd, Thistle Tools, Bentley and Burn, Overdraft Fee, Hopburn Ltd, Bits & Bats, Essentials.

57 WOOD BANK RECONCILIATION

The bank statement and cash book for Wood is shown below.

Money Bags Bank PLC
52 Oak Road, Timperley, SK10 8LR

To: Wood Ltd   Account No: 47013799   23 June 20XX
Statement of Account

Date 20XX	Detail	Paid out £	Paid in £	Balance £	
04 June	Balance b/d			17,640	C
05 June	Bank Giro credit Bradley		1,320	18,960	C
05 June	Bank Giro credit Thanoj		2,450	21,410	C
05 June	Paid in at Money Bags bank PLC		9,420	30,830	C
11 June	Cheque 110341	1,540		29,290	C
12 June	BACS payment Southwell	820		28,470	C
13 June	Cheque 110343	750		27,720	C
15 June	Cheque 110344	570		27,150	C
17 June	Interest earned		80	27,230	C
20 June	Direct debit Blundell	400		26,830	C
23 June	BACS payment Bore	250		26,580	C
23 June	Cheque 110346	740		25,840	C

D = Debit   C = Credit

Cash book

Date 20XX	Details	Bank £	Date 20XX	Cheque number	Details	Bank £
01 June	Balance b/d	17,640				
03 June	Bradley	1,320	04 June	110341	Carr	1,540
03 June	Cash sales	9,420	04 June	110342	Ramsden	980
03 June	Thanoj	2,450	04 June	110343	Coulson	750
21 June	Cash sales	7,430	04 June	110344	Brodie	570
21 June	Devitt	1,990	04 June	110345	Jones	550
17 June	Interest earned	80	04 June	110346	Gritton	740
			20 June		Bore	250
			12 June		Southwell	820
			20 June		Direct debit Blundell	400
			23 June		Balance c/d	33,730
		40,330				40,330
24 June	Balance b/d	33,730				

Complete the bank reconciliation statement as at 23 June.

Note: Do not make any entries in the shaded boxes.

Bank reconciliation statement as at 23 June 20XX

Balance per bank statement	
Add:	
Name:	
Name:	
Total to add	
Less:	
Name:	
Name:	
Total to subtract	
Balance as per cash book	

58   PEARSON BANK RECONCILIATION

The bank statement and cash book for Pearson is shown below.

	Money Bags Bank PLC				
To: Pearson Ltd	Account No: 47013799		23 June 20XX		
	Statement of Account				
Date	**Detail**	**Paid out**	**Paid in**	**Balance**	
20XX		£	£	£	
01 June	Balance b/d			1,340	D
02 June	Bank Giro credit Pond		1,890	550	C
02 June	Interest received		5	555	C
02 June	Direct debit McMenemy	1,200		645	D
11 June	Cheque 110123	430		1,075	D
12 June	Paid in to Money Bags bank		840	235	D
13 June	Cheque 110126	75		310	D
15 June	Cheque 110127	270		580	D
17 June	Paid in to Money Bags bank		1,540	960	C
20 June	Direct debit Findus	300		660	C
23 June	Bank charges	25		635	C
23 June	Cheque 110129	740		105	D
	D = Debit C = Credit				

Cash book

Date 20XX	Details	Bank £	Date 20XX	Cheque number	Details	Bank £
01 June	Balance b/d	550	07 June	110123	Connell	430
09 June	Cash sales	840	07 June	110124	Renner	720
14 June	Cash sales	1,540	07 June	110125	Bond	750
22 June	Cunnington	1,730	07 June	110126	Hatton	75
02 June	Interest received	5	07 June	110127	Bull	270
			07 June	110128	Black	135
			07 June	110129	Southall	740
			02 June		McMenemy	1,200
			20 June		Findus	300
			23 June		Bank charges	25
			23 June		Balance c/d	20
		4,665				4,665
24 June	Balance b/d	20				

Complete the bank reconciliation statement as at 23 June.

Note: Do not make any entries in the shaded boxes.

Bank reconciliation statement as at 23 June 20XX

Balance per bank statement	
Add:	
Name:	
Total to add	
Less:	
Name:	
Name:	
Name:	
Total to subtract	
Balance as per cash book	

(b) Show which security procedure listed below Pearson should use to ensure the security of receipts from customers.

	✓
Cash received from customers should be kept in a locked safe until banked	
Cash should be banked on a monthly basis	
Cheques received too late to bank should be posted through the bank's letter box	

59   MCKEOWN BANK RECONCILIATION

The bank statement and cash book for McKeown is shown below.

Money Bags Bank PLC

To: McKeown Ltd   Account No: 47013799   23 June 20XX

Statement of Account

Date 20XX	Detail	Paid out £	Paid in £	Balance £	
01 June	Balance b/d			7,420	C
01 June	Bank Giro credit Pond		180	7,600	C
01 June	Cheque 110156	420		7,180	C
01 June	Interest received		85	7,265	C
11 June	Cheque 110157	430		6,835	C
12 June	Cheque 110158	520		6,315	C
13 June	Cheque 110161	750		5,565	C
15 June	Bank Giro credit Sherwood		640	6,205	C
17 June	Paid in to Money Bags bank		1,200	7,405	C
20 June	Bank Giro credit Coyne		1,630	9,035	C
23 June	Direct debit Wilmott	300		8,735	C
23 June	Interest received		35	8,770	C

D = Debit   C = Credit

Cash book

Date 20XX	Details	Bank £	Date 20XX	Cheque number	Details	Bank £
01 June	Balance b/d	7,180	07 June	110157	Williams	430
12 June	Sherwood	640	07 June	110158	Forecast	520
14 June	Cash sales	1,200	07 June	110159	Beasant	1,240
22 June	Tweedy	860	07 June	110160	Davison	1,420
23 June	Butterwood	440	07 June	110161	Mildenhall	750
01 June	Interest received	85	23 June		Wilmott	300
20 June	Coyne	1,630				
23 June	Interest received	35				
			23 June		Balance c/d	7,410
		12,070				12,070
24 June	Balance b/d	7,410				

Complete the bank reconciliation statement as at 23 June.

Note: Do not make any entries in the shaded boxes.

Bank reconciliation statement as at 23 June 20XX

Balance per bank statement	
Add:	
Name:	
Name:	
Total to add	
Less:	
Name:	
Name:	
Total to subtract	
Balance as per cash book	

(c) Show which security procedure listed below McKeown should use to ensure the security of receipts from customers.

	✓
Cash should be banked on a daily basis	
Cheques should be banked on a monthly basis	
Cheques received too late to bank should be posted through the bank's letter box	

PREPARE AND RECONCILE SALES/PURCHASE LEDGER CONTROL ACCOUNTS

60 MONSTER MUNCHIES

This is a summary of transactions with customers of Monster Munchies during the month of June.

(a) **Show whether each entry will be a debit or credit in the Sales ledger control account in the General ledger.**

Details	Amount £	Debit ✓	Credit ✓
Balance of receivables at 1 June	48,000		
Goods sold on credit	12,415		
Receipts from credit customers	22,513		
Discount allowed	465		
Sales returns from credit customers	320		

(b) **What will be the balance brought down on 1 July on the above account?**

✓

Dr £37,117	
Cr £37,117	
Dr £83,713	
Cr £83,713	
Dr £58,883	
Cr £58,883	

The following debit balances were in the subsidiary (sales) ledger on 1 July.

	£
XXX Ltd	21,300
Brittle Homes Ltd	5,376
Colin and Campbell	333
Bashford Incorporated	1,733
Mainstreet Homes	3,426
Shamrock Interiors	4,629

(c) **Reconcile the balances shown above with the sales ledger control account balance you have calculated in part (a).**

	£
Sales ledger control account balance as at 30 June	
Total of subsidiary (sales) ledger accounts as at 30 June	
Difference	

(d) **What may have caused the difference you calculated in part (c)?**

✓

Sales returns may have been omitted from the subsidiary ledger.	
Discounts allowed may have been omitted from the subsidiary ledger.	
Sales returns may have been entered in the subsidiary ledger twice.	
Discounts allowed may have been entered in the subsidiary ledger twice.	

It is important to reconcile the sales ledger control account on a regular basis.

(e) **Which of the following statements is true?**

	✓
Reconciliation of the sales ledger control account assures managers that the amount showing as owed to suppliers is correct.	
Reconciliation of the sales ledger control account assures managers that the amount showing as outstanding from customers is correct.	
Reconciliation of the sales ledger control account will show if a purchase invoice has been omitted from the purchase ledger.	
Reconciliation of the sales ledger control account will show if a purchase invoice has been omitted from the sales ledger .	

61   JACK'S BOX

This is a summary of transactions with customers of Jack's Box during the month of April.

(a)   **Show whether each entry will be a debit or a credit in the Sales ledger control account in the General ledger.**

Details	Amount £	Debit ✓	Credit ✓
Balance of receivables at 1 April	60,589		
Goods sold on credit	26,869		
Payments received from credit customers	29,411		
Discount allowed	598		
Goods returned from credit customers	1,223		

(b)   **What will be the balance brought down on 1 May on the above account?**

	✓
Dr £55,030	
Cr £55,030	
Dr £56,226	
Cr £56,226	
Dr £52,584	
Cr £52,584	

The following debit balances were in the subsidiary (receivables) ledger on 1 May.

	£
Olsen & Lane	19,455
Frith Ltd	625
Hodgetts & Co	412
Geevor plc	17,623
Trevaskis Farm Ltd	16,888

(c)   **Reconcile the balances shown above with the sales ledger control account balance you have calculated in part (b).**

	£
Sales Ledger control account balances as at 30 April	
Total of subsidiary (sales) ledger accounts as at 30 April	
Difference	

(d)   **What may have caused the difference you calculated in part (c)?**

	✓
Sales returns may have been omitted from the subsidiary ledger	
Discounts allowed have been omitted from the subsidiary ledger	
Sales returns have been entered into the subsidiary ledger twice	
Discounts allowed have been entered into subsidiary ledger twice	

It is important to reconcile the sales ledger control account on a regular basis.

(e)   **Which of the following statements is true?**

	✓
Reconciliation of the sales ledger control account will show if a purchase invoice has been omitted from the purchases ledger.	
Reconciliation of the sales ledger control account will show if a sales invoice has been omitted from the purchases ledger.	
Reconciliation of the sales ledger control account assures managers that the amount showing due to suppliers is correct.	
Reconciliation of the sales ledger control account assures managers that the amount showing due from customers is correct.	

62 CILLA'S SINKS

This is a summary of transactions with suppliers of Cilla's Sinks during the month of June.

(a) **Show whether each entry will be a debit or credit in the Purchase ledger control account in the General ledger.**

Details	Amount £	Debit ✓	Credit ✓
Balance of payables at 1 June	52,150		
Goods bought on credit	19,215		
Payments made to credit suppliers	19,073		
Discount received	284		
Goods returned to credit suppliers	1,023		

(b) **What will be the balance brought down on 1 July on the above account?**

	✓
Dr £51,553	
Cr £51,553	
Dr £50,985	
Cr £50,985	
Dr £50,701	
Cr £50,701	

The following credit balances were in the subsidiary (purchase) ledger on 1 July.

	£
BWF Ltd	19,563
All Parts Ltd	10,207
Hove Albion	4,501
Barton Groves	6,713
Cambridge Irons	5,913
Outside Arenas	5,111

(c) **Reconcile the balances shown above with the purchase ledger control account balance you have calculated in part (a).**

	£
Purchase ledger control account balance as at 30 June	
Total of subsidiary (purchase) ledger accounts as at 30 June	
Difference	

(d)   **What may have caused the difference you calculated in part (b)?**

	✓
Goods returned may have been omitted from the subsidiary ledger.	
Discounts received may have been omitted from the subsidiary ledger.	
Goods returned may have been entered in the subsidiary ledger twice.	
Discounts received may have been entered in the subsidiary ledger twice.	

It is important to reconcile the purchase ledger control account on a regular basis.

(e)   **Which of the following statements is true?**

	✓
Reconciliation of the purchase ledger control account will help to identify any supplier invoices that have been omitted in error.	
Reconciliation of the purchase ledger control account will show if a sales invoice has been omitted from the purchase ledger.	
Reconciliation of the purchase ledger control account will show if a sales invoice has been omitted from the sales ledger.	
Reconciliation of the purchase ledger control account will help to identify any discounts allowed that have been omitted in error.	

63   VIK'S TRICKS

This is a summary of transactions with customers of Vik's Tricks during the month of June.

(a)   **Show whether each entry will be a debit or credit in the Sales ledger control account in the General ledger.**

Details	Amount £	Debit ✓	Credit ✓
Balance of receivables at 1 June	58,120		
Goods sold on credit	20,013		
Receipts from credit customers	22,327		
Discount allowed	501		
Sales returns from credit customers	970		

(b) **What will be the balance brought down on 1 July on the above account?**

	✓
Dr £58,963	
Cr £58,963	
Dr £57,277	
Cr £57,277	
Dr £54,335	
Cr £54,335	

The following debit balances were in the subsidiary (sales) ledger on 1 July.

	£
Woffel Homes	21,026
Perfect Rooms Ltd	14,709
Brighton Dwellings Ltd	7,864
Grosvenor Homes	3,198
Oxford Designs	3,011
Indoor Delights	5,497

(c) **Reconcile the balances shown above with the sales ledger control account balance you have calculated in part (a).**

	£
Sales ledger control account balance as at 30 June	
Total of subsidiary (sales) ledger accounts as at 30 June	
Difference	

(d) **What may have caused the difference you calculated in part (b)?**

	✓
Discounts allowed may have been entered in the subsidiary ledger twice.	
Discounts allowed may have been omitted from the subsidiary ledger.	
Sales returns may have been entered in the subsidiary ledger twice.	
Sales returns may have been omitted from the subsidiary ledger.	

It is important to reconcile the sales ledger control account on a regular basis.

(e)   **Which of the following statements is true?**

	✓
Reconciliation of the sales ledger control account will help to identify any customer invoices that have been omitted in error.	
Reconciliation of the sales ledger control account will show if a purchase invoice has been omitted from the sales ledger.	
Reconciliation of the sales ledger control account will show if a purchase invoice has been omitted from the purchase ledger.	
Reconciliation of the sales ledger control account will help to identify any discounts received that have been omitted in error.	

64   ZHANG

When Zhang came to reconcile his SLCA with his list of balances on the sales ledger, he found that they did not match. The SLCA had a balance of £65,830 and the list of balances totalled £65,090. Upon further investigation, he discovered that the following errors had been made:

1   The sales day book had been incorrectly totalled and had been overcast by £1,200.

2   A contra of £800 had been made in the SLCA, but had not been recorded in the sales ledger.

3   A credit note of £130 had been posted twice in the sales ledger.

4   A discount given of £210 had only been recorded in the sales ledger.

(a)   **Update the SLCA and list of balances to make sure that the two agree.**

SLCA

Details	Amount £	Details	Amount £
Balance b/d	65,830		
		Balance c/d	
Balance b/d			

List of balances:

	£
Total	65,090
Revised total	

(b)   **Show whether the following statements are true or false:**

	True ✓	False ✓
An aged trade receivables analysis is used when chasing customers for outstanding payments.		
An aged trade receivables analysis is sent to credit customers when payments are being requested.		

65   HANDYSIDE

When Handyside came to reconcile his PLCA with his list of balances on the purchases ledger, he found that they did not match. The PLCA had a balance of £25,360 and the list of balances totalled £26,000. Upon further investigation, he discovered that the following errors had been made:

1   In the list of balances, a purchase of £2,400 had been entered at the net amount.

2   Returns of £350 had not been applied to the purchases ledger.

3   An invoice for £600 plus VAT had not been posted in the general ledger yet.

4   Returns of £120 were missing from the PLCA.

5   An invoice for £340 had been entered into the purchases ledger as £430.

(a)   **Update the PLCA and list of balances to make sure that the two agree.**

PLCA

Details	Amount £	Details	Amount £
		Balance b/d	25,360
Balance c/d			
		Balance b/d	

List of balances:

	£
Total	26,000
Revised total	

(b) **Show whether the following statements are true or false:**

	True ✓	False ✓
The purchases ledger control account enables a business to see how much is owed to individual suppliers		
The purchases ledger control account total should reconcile to the total of the list of supplier balances in the purchases ledger		

VAT CONTROL ACCOUNT

66 BENJAMIN BISHOP

The following is an extract from Benjamin Bishop's books of prime entry.

Totals for quarter

Sales day-book		Purchases day-book	
Net:	£188,000	Net:	£101,200
VAT:	£37,600	VAT:	£20,240
Gross:	£225,600	Gross:	£121,440
Sales returns day-book		**Purchases returns day-book**	
Net:	£3,200	Net:	£6,320
VAT:	£640	VAT:	£1,264
Gross:	£3,840	Gross:	£7,584
Cash book			
Net cash sales:	£520		
VAT:	£104		
Gross cash sales:	£624		

(a) **What will be the entries in the VAT control account to record the VAT transactions in the quarter?**

VAT control

Details	Amount £	Details	Amount £

Picklist: Cash sales, Purchases, Purchases returns, Sales, Sales returns, VAT

The VAT return has been completed and shows an amount due to HM Revenue and Customs of £18,088.

(b) **Is the VAT return correct?**   Yes/No

67   RING RING TELEPHONE

The following is an extract from Ring Ring Telephone's books of prime entry.

		Totals for quarter	
Sales day-book		**Purchases day-book**	
Net:	£153,000	Net:	£81,000
VAT:	£30,600	VAT:	£16,200
Gross:	£183,600	Gross:	£97,200
Sales returns day-book		**Purchases returns day-book**	
Net:	£1,800	Net:	£5,800
VAT:	£360	VAT:	£1,160
Gross:	£2,160	Gross:	£6,960
Cash book			
Net cash sales:	£240		
VAT:	£48		
Gross cash sales:	£288		

(a)   **What will be the entries in the VAT control account to record the VAT transactions in the quarter?**

VAT control

Details	Amount £	Details	Amount £

Picklist: Cash sales, Purchases, Purchases returns, Sales, Sales returns, VAT.

The VAT return has been completed and shows an amount owing from HM Revenue and Customs of £15,248.

(b)   **Is the VAT return correct?**   Yes/No

68 JO'S JOINERS

The following is an extract from Jo's Joiners books of prime entry.

Totals for quarter			
Sales day book		**Purchases day book**	
Net:	£156,000	Net:	£105,000
VAT:	£31,200	VAT:	£21,000
Gross:	£187,200	Gross:	£126,000
Sales returns day book		**Purchases returns day book**	
Net:	£3,600	Net:	£5,440
VAT:	£720	VAT:	£1,088
Gross:	£4,320	Gross:	£6,528
Cash Book			
Net cash sales:	£600		
VAT:	£120		
Gross cash sales:	£720		

Picklist: Cash sales, Purchases, Purchases returns, Sales, Sales returns, VAT.

(a) **What will be the entries in the VAT control account to record the VAT transactions in the quarter?**

VAT Control

Details	Amount £	Details	Amount £

The VAT return has been completed and shows an amount owed to HM Revenue and Customs of £10,688.

(b) **Is the VAT return correct?**   Yes/No

69 PHILIP'S CABINS

The following is an extract from Philip's Cabins books of prime entry.

Totals for quarter			
Sales day-book		**Purchases day-book**	
Net:	£179,800	Net:	£100,200
VAT:	£35,960	VAT:	£20,040
Gross:	£215,760	Gross:	£120,240
Sales returns day-book		**Purchases returns day-book**	
Net:	£3,000	Net:	£5,720
VAT:	£600	VAT:	£1,144
Gross:	£3,600	Gross:	£6,864
Cash book			
Net cash sales:	£560		
VAT:	£112		
Gross cash sales:	£672		

(a) **What will be the entries in the VAT control account to record the VAT transactions in the quarter?**

VAT control

Details	Amount £	Details	Amount £

Picklist: Cash sales, Purchases, Purchases returns, Sales, Sales returns, VAT.

The VAT return has been completed and shows an amount due to HM Revenue and Customs of £14,540.

(b) **Is the VAT return correct?**   Yes/No

70   DISLEY

(a)   **Show whether each item is a debit or credit balance in the VAT control account by copying the amount into the correct column.**

	£	*Debit*	*Credit*
VAT total in the sales day book	65,420		
VAT total in the purchases day book	21,340		
VAT total in the sales returns day book	480		
VAT balance brought forward, owed to HMRC	24,910		
VAT on irrecoverable debts	830		
VAT on petty cash expenses paid	210		

The VAT return has been completed and shows an amount due to HM Revenue and Customs of £67,740.

(b)   **Is the VAT return correct?** Yes/No

71   KERR

(a)   **Show whether each item is a debit or credit balance in the VAT control account by copying the amount into the correct column.**

	£	*Debit*	*Credit*
VAT total in the purchase returns day book	1,320		
VAT on cash purchases	2,670		
VAT on the sale of equipment	970		
VAT refund received from HMRC	2,580		
VAT on cash sales	5,680		
VAT balance brought forward, due from HMRC	2,580		

The VAT return has been completed and shows an amount due to HM Revenue and Customs of £5,300.

(b)   **Is the VAT return correct?** Yes/No

72   NEILSON

(a)   **Show whether each item is a debit or credit balance in the VAT control account by copying the amount into the correct column.**

	£	*Debit*	*Credit*
VAT total in the sales day book	54,670		
VAT total in the purchases day book	26,340		
VAT total in the sales returns day book	1,240		
VAT total in the purchases returns day book	760		
VAT on sale of equipment	3,210		
VAT on petty cash expenses paid	500		
VAT balance brought forward, owed to HMRC	42,180		
VAT on irrecoverable debts	430		
VAT paid to HMRC during the period	32,150		
VAT on cash sales	6,540		
VAT on cash purchases	7,520		

The VAT return has been completed and shows an amount due to HM Revenue and Customs of £39,180.

(b)   **Is the VAT return correct?** Yes/No

THE BANKING SYSTEM

73   COLBECK

Show whether each of the statements below is true or false.

An organisation's document retention policy should contain a requirement for banking documents to be kept for a minimum of 7 years.

True/False

A standing order will allow an organisation to make payments of fixed amounts.

True/False

When a payment is made via cheque, the words on the cheque must match the amount shown in figures in order for the cheque to be valid.

True/False

Before accepting a cheque payment, an organisation should ask the bank if there are sufficient funds in the customer's bank account.

True/False

74   BLOSSOM BLOOMS

Blossom Blooms receives payment from customers and makes payments to suppliers in a variety of ways.

(a)   **Select FOUR checks that DO NOT have to be made on each of the two payment methods shown below when received from customers.**

Checks to be made	Cheque ✓	Telephone credit card payment ✓
Check expiry date		
Check issue number		
Check not post dated		
Check security number		
Check words and figures match		
Check card has not been tampered with		

(b)   **Show whether each of the statements below is true or false.**

When Blossom Blooms makes payments to suppliers by debit card, the amount paid affects the bank current account

True/False

When Blossom Blooms makes payments to suppliers by credit card, the amount paid affects the bank current account

True/False

75   BELLA BAKERS

Banks and building societies offer many similar services.

(a)   **From the list below select TWO services that are not generally offered by building societies.**

Service	Not offered by building societies ✓
Foreign currency	
Loan	
Overdraft	
Safe custody	
Savings account	
Telephone banking	

(b) **Show whether the following statements are true or false.**

A bank cheque paid into a building society has to pass through the clearing system

True/False

A building society cheque paid into a bank has to pass through the clearing system

True/False

It is important to understand that banking documents need to be retained by an organisation so that Accountants, HM Revenue and Customs, and other organisations can access them when required.

(c) **Which THREE of the documents below are banking documents that must be retained by Bella Bakers?**

	✓
Aged receivable analysis	
Aged payable analysis	
Paying in slip stubs	
Credit cards	
Debit cards	
Bank statements	
Cheque book stubs	
Customer invoices	

76 PETE'S PARROTS

Pete's Parrots receives payment from customers and makes payments to suppliers in a variety of ways.

(a) **Select TWO checks that have to be made on each of the two payment methods shown below when received from customers.**

Checks to be made	Cheque ✓	Telephone credit card payment ✓
Check expiry date		
Check issue number		
Check not post dated		
Check security number		
Check words and figures match		
Check card has not been tampered with		

(b) **Show whether each of the statements below is true or false.**

When Pete's Parrots makes payments to suppliers by credit card, the amount does not leave the bank current account immediately

True/False

When Pete's Parrots makes payments to suppliers by debit card, the amount paid affects the bank current account

True/False

77 BANKS

Banks and building societies offer many similar services.

(a) **From the list below select TWO services that are offered by both banks AND building societies.**

Service	Offered by BOTH banks and building societies ✓
Overdraft	
Savings account	
Foreign currency	
Safe custody	

(b) **Show whether the following statements are true or false:**

	True ✓	False ✓
A building society cheque does not have to be passed to the bank of the issuer before the money becomes available.		
A bank cheque paid into a building society has to pass through the clearing system.		
A bank cheque does not have to be passed to the bank of the issuer before the money becomes available.		
A building society cheque paid into a bank has to pass through the clearing system.		

(c) **Which TWO of the documents below are banking documents that must be retained?**

	✓
Petty cash VAT invoices	
Cheque book stubs	
Supplier statement reconciliations	
Aged payables analysis	
Overdraft agreement	
Sales invoices	

78   KITE LTD

Kite Ltd receives payments from customers and makes payments to suppliers in a variety of ways.

(a)   **Select TWO checks that have to be made on each of the two payment methods shown below when received from customers.**

Checks to be made	BACS receipt ✓	Cheque ✓
Check security number		
Check remittance advice		
Check crossed with 'Account Payee'		
Check payer is a customer		
Check signature has been made		
Check card has not been tampered with		

(b)   **Show whether each of the statements below is true or false.**

	True ✓	False ✓
When Kite Ltd receives a remittance advice from a customer, the amount will already be in Kite Ltd's bank current account.		
When Kite Ltd makes a payment to a supplier by BACS, the amount paid affects the bank current account.		

79   BUILDING SOCIETY

Banks and building societies offer many similar services.

(a)   **From the list below select FOUR services that are offered by building societies.**

Service	Offered by building societies ✓
Foreign currency	
Loan	
Overdraft	
Safe custody	
Savings account	
Telephone banking	

(b)   **Show whether the following statements are true or false.**

A bank cheque paid into a building society does not have to pass through the clearing system

True/False

A building society cheque paid into a bank has to pass through the clearing system

True/False

A bank cheque has to be passed to the bank of the issuer before the money becomes available

True/False

A building society cheque does not have to be passed to the bank of the issuer before the money becomes available

True/False

It is important to understand that banking documents need to be retained by an organisation so that Accountants, HM Revenue and Customs, and other organisations can access them when required.

(c)   **Which TWO of the documents below are banking documents that must be retained?**

	✓
Aged receivable analysis	
Aged payable analysis	
Cash book	
Credit cards	
Debit cards	
Bank Statements	
Cheque book stubs	
Customer invoices	

80   GATES

Gates receives payment from customers and makes payments to suppliers in a variety of ways.

(a)   **Select FOUR checks that DO NOT have to be made on each of the two payment methods shown below when received from customers.**

Checks to be made	Cheque ✓	Telephone credit card payment ✓
Check expiry date		
Check issue number		
Check not post dated		
Check security number		
Check words and figures match		
Check card has not been tampered with		

(b)   **Show whether each of the statements below is true or false.**

When Gates makes payments to suppliers by credit card, the amount paid effects the bank current account

True/False

When Gates makes payments to suppliers by debit card, the amount paid affects the bank current account

True/False

81   METHODS OF PAYMENT

Match the payment need with the most likely method of payment to be used.

Replacement batteries for office clock	CHAPS payment
Payment to complete the purchase of a new building, which needs to clear today	Debit/Credit card
Fixed monthly charge for rent	Direct debit
Payment for telephone bill, which fluctuates monthly	Cheque
Payment to regular supplier	Petty cash
Online purchase of computer equipment	Standing order

82   METHODS OF PAYMENT 2

Match the payment with the description below

Standing order	A payment made for regular bills which fluctuate in value
Bank loan	A facility allowing customers to deposit cash and cheques after bank opening hours
Direct debit	A regular payment for a fixed amount
Bank overdraft	A facility allowing customers to borrow money on a long term basis
Night safe	A facility allowing customers to borrow money on a short term flexible basis

Section 2

ANSWERS TO PRACTICE QUESTIONS

THE JOURNAL

1   INTREPID INTERIORS

Account name	Amount £	Debit ✓	Credit ✓
Cash at bank	7,250	✓	
Bank Loan	5,000		✓
Capital	10,625		✓
Motor vehicles	4,750	✓	
Insurances	575	✓	
Stationery	300	✓	
Sundry expenses	225	✓	
Motor expenses	135	✓	
Advertising	990	✓	
Rent and rates	1,400	✓	
Journal to record the opening entries of new business			

2   BEDROOM BITS

Account name	Amount £	Debit ✓	Credit ✓
Cash	325	✓	
Cash at bank	9,625	✓	
Capital	22,008		✓
Fixtures and fittings	4,250	✓	
Insurance	1,050	✓	
Loan from bank	15,000		✓
Miscellaneous expenses	413	✓	
Motor vehicle	19,745	✓	
Office expenses	350	✓	
Rent and rates	1,250	✓	
-Journal to record the opening entries of new business			

3   GARDEN GATES

Account name	Amount £	Debit ✓	Credit ✓
Cash	450	✓	
Cash at bank	11,125	✓	
Capital	28,941		✓
Plant and machinery	5,050	✓	
Insurance	990	✓	
Loan from bank	12,500		✓
General office expenses	378	✓	
Motor vehicle	20,755	✓	
Advertising	893	✓	
Rent and rates	1,800	✓	
Journal to record the opening entries of new business			

PAYROLL

4   IVANO

(a)

	Amount £
Net pay (2,400 – 480 – 245 – 80)	1,595

Note: The net pay is the gross pay less all the EMPLOYEE'S deductions. Employer's NIC is not part of this calculation.

(b)

	Amount £
Wages and salaries (Employer's expense) (2,400 Gross pay + 255 Employer's NIC)	2,655

(c)

	Amount £
Liabilities (HMRC and Pension) HMRC = 480 + 245 + 255 = 980 Pension = 80	1,060

5 ANNA

(a)

	Amount £
Net pay (1,400 – 280 – 125 – 60)	935

Note: The net pay is the gross pay less all the EMPLOYEE'S deductions. Employer's NIC is not part of this calculation.

(b)

	Amount £
Wages and salaries (Employer's expense) (1,400 Gross pay + 135 Employer's NIC + 70 Employer pension contributions)	1,605

(c)

	Amount £
Liabilities (HMRC and pension) HMRC = 280 + 125 + 135 = 540 Pension = 130	600

6 GROSS PAY 1

Item	Included in gross pay ✓	Not included in gross pay ✓
Salary	✓	
Employer's NIC		✓
Overtime	✓	
Bonus	✓	
Expenses reimbursement		✓
PAYE		✓

Gross pay is the amount the employee has earned from working for the company and therefore includes salary, overtime bonuses, shift payments. Employer's NIC is added to gross pay in order to calculate the total wages expense for the company. While the employee will be reimbursed for expenses, these are not part of the pay earned by the individual. This is simply paying the individual back for expenses they have personally incurred on behalf of the business.

7 GROSS PAY 2

Item	Included in gross pay ✓	Not included in gross pay ✓
Salary	✓	
Employer's NIC		✓
Commission	✓	
Employee's NIC		✓
Pension contribution		✓
PAYE		✓

Gross pay is the amount the employee has earned from working for the company and therefore includes salary, overtime bonuses, shift payments. Employer's NIC is added to gross pay in order to calculate the total wages expense for the company.

8 A POCKET FULL OF POSES

(i)

Account name	Amount £	Debit ✓	Credit ✓
Wages expense	17,755	✓	
Wages control	17,755		✓

(ii)

Account name	Amount £	Debit ✓	Credit ✓
HM Revenue and Customs	7,500		✓
Wages control	7,500	✓	

(iii)

Account name	Amount £	Debit ✓	Credit ✓
Bank	8,405		✓
Wages control	8,405	✓	

(iv)

Account name	Amount £	Debit ✓	Credit ✓
Pension	1,850		✓
Wages control	1,850	✓	

Proof (not required to answer the question correctly):

Wages control

HM Revenue and Customs	7,500	Wages expense	17,755
Bank	8,405		
Pension	1,850		
	———		———
	16,755		17,755
	———		———

9   RHYME TIME

(i)

Account name	Amount £	Debit ✓	Credit ✓
Wages expense	11,915	✓	
Wages control	11,915		✓

(ii)

Account name	Amount £	Debit ✓	Credit ✓
HM Revenue and Customs	5,026		✓
Wages control	5,026	✓	

(iii)

Account name	Amount £	Debit ✓	Credit ✓
Bank	5,739		✓
Wages control	5,739	✓	

(iv)

Account name	Amount £	Debit ✓	Credit ✓
Pension	1,150		✓
Wages control	1,150	✓	

Wages control

HM Revenue and Customs	5,026	Wages expense	11,915
Bank	5,739		
Pension	1,150		
	———		———
	11,915		11,915
	———		———

10 DOWN & OUT

(i)

Account name	Amount £	Debit ✓	Credit ✓
Wages expense	9,567	✓	
Wages control	9,567		✓

(ii)

Account name	Amount £	Debit ✓	Credit ✓
HM Revenue and Customs	3,673		✓
Wages control	3,673	✓	

(iii)

Account name	Amount £	Debit ✓	Credit ✓
Bank	5,469		✓
Wages control	5,469	✓	

(iv)

Account name	Amount £	Debit ✓	Credit ✓
Trade union	425		✓
Wages control	425	✓	

Proof (not required to answer the question correctly):

Wages control			
HM Revenue and Customs	3,673	Wages expense	9,567
Bank	5,469		
Trade union	425		
	———		———
	9,567		9,567
	———		———

11 DEV'S

(i)

Account name	Amount £	Debit ✓	Credit ✓
Wages expense	13,963	✓	
Wages control	13,963		✓

(ii)

Account name	Amount £	Debit ✓	Credit ✓
HM Revenue and Customs	6,251		✓
Wages control	6,251	✓	

(iii)

Account name	Amount £	Debit ✓	Credit ✓
Bank	7,212		✓
Wages control	7,212	✓	

(iv)

Account name	Amount £	Debit ✓	Credit ✓
Trade union	500		✓
Wages control	500	✓	

Proof (not required to answer the question correctly):

Wages control

HM Revenue and Customs	6,251	Wages expense	13,963
Bank	7,212		
Trade Union	500		
	13,963		13,963

IRRECOVERABLE DEBTS AND TYPES OF ERROR

12   BEDROOM BITS 2

Account name	Amount £	Debit ✓	Credit ✓
Irrecoverable debts	2,000	✓	
VAT	400	✓	
Sales ledger control	2,400		✓

13   GARDEN GATES 2

Account name	Amount £	Debit ✓	Credit ✓
Irrecoverable debts	2,600	✓	
VAT	520	✓	
Sales ledger control	3,120		✓

14   CHESTNUT

SLCA

Details	Amount £	Details	Amount £
Balance b/d	46,000	Contra	4,000
		Balance c/d	42,000
	46,000		**46,000**
Balance b/d	42,000		

PLCA

Details	Amount £	Details	Amount £
Contra	4,000	Balance b/d	31,000
Balance c/d	27,000		
	31,000		**31,000**
		Balance b/d	27,000

15   ALLEN

SLCA

Details	Amount £	Details	Amount £
Balance b/d	56,000	Contra	11,000
		Balance c/d	45,000
	56,000		**56,000**
Balance b/d	45,000		

PLCA

Details	Amount £	Details	Amount £
Contra	11,000	Balance b/d	49,000
Balance c/d	38,000		
	49,000		**49,000**
		Balance b/d	38,000

16 ERROR TYPES 1

Error in the general ledger	Error disclosed by the trial balance	Error NOT disclosed by the trial balance
Incorrectly calculating the balance on the Motor Vehicles account.	✓	
Recording a receipt for commission received in the bank interest received account.		✓
Recording a bank receipt for bank interest received on the debit side of both the bank account and the bank interest received account.	✓	
Recording supplier invoices on the debit side of the purchase ledger control account and the credit side of the purchases account.		✓
Recording a payment by cheque to a payable in the purchase ledger control account only.	✓	
Recording a bank payment of £124 for insurance as £142 in the insurance account and £124 in the bank account.	✓	

17 ERROR TYPES 2

Error in the general ledger	Error disclosed by the trial balance	Error NOT disclosed by the trial balance
Recording a bank receipt for rent received on the credit side of both the bank account and rent received account.	✓	
Recording a payment for new machinery in the equipment hire account.		✓
Recording a purchase return on the credit side of the purchase ledger control account and the debit side of the purchase returns account.		✓
Incorrectly calculating the balance on the bank interest received account.	✓	
Recording a payment by cheque to a payable in the bank account only.	✓	
Recording a bank payment of £120 for stationery as £210 in both accounts.		✓

18   ERROR TYPES 3

Error in the general ledger	Type of error
Recording a bank receipt for rent received on the credit side of both the bank account and rent received account.	Two entries on one side
Recording a payment for new machinery in the equipment hire account.	Error of principle
Recording a purchase return on the credit side of the purchase ledger control account and the debit side of the purchase returns account.	Reversal of entries

19   ERROR TYPES 4

Error in the general ledger	Type of error
Recording a payment by cheque to a payable in the bank account only.	Single entry
Recording a bank payment of £100 for stationery as £210 in both accounts.	Error of original entry
Recording a receipt for commission received in the bank interest received account.	Error of commission

20   ERROR TYPES 5

Error in the general ledger	Type of error
A credit sale made at the month end was not recorded.	Error of omission
Recording a bank payment of £120 for stationery as £210 in the stationery account and correctly in the bank account.	Transposition error
Recording a receipt for commission received in the PLCA.	Error of principle

21   PRINCIPLES

(a)

Recording a bank payment for rent on the debit side of the office equipment account.	✓

(b)

Recording rent received as a debit in the rent account.	✓

22   EXTRACTION

(a)

Totalling the sales day book correctly but entering into the SLCA as a credit balance.	✓

(b)

Posting a £200 invoice for electricity as £210 in both the electricity and bank account.	✓

ERRORS

23   BANK ERROR

(i)

Account name	Amount £	Debit ✓	Credit ✓
Repairs	750	✓	
Bank	750		✓

(ii)

Account name	Amount £	Debit ✓	Credit ✓
Repairs	750	✓	
Bank	750		✓

24   RENT ERROR

(i)

Account name	Amount £	Debit ✓	Credit ✓
Bank	500	✓	
Rent received	500		✓

(ii)

Account name	Amount £	Debit ✓	Credit ✓
Bank	500	✓	
Rent received	500		✓

25   GAS ERROR

Account name	Amount £	Debit ✓	Credit ✓
Gas expenses	300	✓	
Electricity expenses	300		✓

26   BUILDING ERROR

Account name	Amount £	Debit ✓	Credit ✓
Suspense	360,000	✓	
Bank	360,000		✓

27 SALES ERROR

Account name	Amount £	Debit ✓	Credit ✓
Sales	2,000	✓	
VAT	2,000		✓

BALANCING THE TRIAL BALANCE AND CORRECTION OF ERRORS

28 CB INTERIORS

(i)

Account name	Amount £	Debit ✓	Credit ✓
Purchase ledger control	960	✓	

(ii)

Account name	Amount £	Debit ✓	Credit ✓
Purchase ledger control	9,600		✓

(iii)

Account name	Amount £	Debit ✓	Credit ✓
Suspense	8,640	✓	

29 ROGER DODGER

(i)

Account name	Amount £	Debit ✓	Credit ✓
VAT	1,680	✓	

(ii)

Account name	Amount £	Debit ✓	Credit ✓
VAT	1,320		✓

(iii)

Account name	Amount £	Debit ✓	Credit ✓
Suspense	360		✓

30   A CUT ABOVE

(i)

Account name	Amount £	Debit ✓	Credit ✓
Purchase ledger control	6,182		✓

(ii)

Account name	Amount £	Debit ✓	Credit ✓
Purchase ledger control	5,952	✓	

(iii)

Account name	Amount £	Debit ✓	Credit ✓
Suspense	230	✓	

31   RESTCO

(i)

Account name	Amount £	Debit ✓	Credit ✓
Sales	8,080	✓	

(ii)

Account name	Amount £	Debit ✓	Credit ✓
Sales	8,800		✓

(iii)

Account name	Amount £	Debit ✓	Credit ✓
Suspense	720	✓	

32   JOHNNY JOINER

(a)

Account name	Amount £	Debit ✓	Credit ✓
Suspense	14,363		✓

(b)

Account name	Amount £	Debit ✓	Credit ✓
Suspense	14,363	✓	
Sales	14,363		✓

33   BUCKLEY DRAINS

(a)

Account name	Amount £	Debit ✓	Credit ✓
Suspense	10,805		✓

(b)

Account name	Amount £	Debit ✓	Credit ✓
Suspense	10,805	✓	
PLCA	10,805		✓

(c)   Show one reason for maintaining the journal

	✓
To correct errors only	
To correct errors and record transactions that have not been recorded in any other book of prime entry	✓
To record transactions from every other book of prime entry.	

34   MENDONCA

(a)

Account name	Amount £	Debit ✓	Credit ✓
Suspense	1,980		✓

(b)

Account name	Amount £	Debit ✓	Credit ✓
Suspense	1,980	✓	
Wages	900	✓	
Bank	2,880		✓

35   BEASANT

(a)

Account name	Amount £	Debit ✓	Credit ✓
Suspense	15,000		✓

(b)

Account name	Amount £	Debit ✓	Credit ✓
Suspense	15,000	✓	
Sales	12,500		✓
VAT	2,500		✓

(c) **Show one reason for maintaining the journal**

	✓
To detect fraud	
To record non-regular transactions	✓
To record goods sold on credit	

POSTING JOURNAL ENTRIES TO LEDGER ACCOUNTS

36   PAT'S CAFE

Bank interest paid

Details	Amount £	Details	Amount £
Bank Interest Received	114		

Bank interest received

Details	Amount £	Details	Amount £
		Bank Interest Paid	114

Suspense

Details	Amount £	Details	Amount £
Motor vehicles	4,500	Balance b/d	4,350
		Insurance	150

Insurance

Details	Amount £	Details	Amount £
Suspense	150		

Motor vehicles

Details	Amount £	Details	Amount £
		Suspense	4,500

37 TWINKLE'S TRINKETS

Motor expenses

Details	Amount £	Details	Amount £
Suspense	324		

Repairs and renewals

Details	Amount £	Details	Amount £
		Suspense	1,100

Suspense

Details	Amount £	Details	Amount £
Repairs and renewals	1,100	Balance b/d	776
		Motor expenses	324

Rent received

Details	Amount £	Details	Amount £
		Rent payable	500

Rent payable

Details	Amount £	Details	Amount £
Rent received	500		

38   SPARKS AND MENCER

Heat and light

Details	Amount £	Details	Amount £
		Suspense	545

Rates

Details	Amount £	Details	Amount £
Suspense	786		

Suspense

Details	Amount £	Details	Amount £
Balance b/d	241	Rates	786
Heat and light	545		

Loan interest expense

Details	Amount £	Details	Amount £
Bank interest received	269		

Bank interest received

Details	Amount £	Details	Amount £
		Loan interest expense	269

39 PIRATE PETE'S

Commission paid

Details	Amount £	Details	Amount £
Commission received	450		

Commission received

Details	Amount £	Details	Amount £
		Commission paid	450

Suspense

Details	Amount £	Details	Amount £
Plant and machinery	2,424	Balance b/d	1,935
		Light and heat	489

Light and heat

Details	Amount £	Details	Amount £
Suspense	489		

Plant and machinery

Details	Amount £	Details	Amount £
		Suspense	2,424

RE-DRAFT THE TRIAL BALANCE

40 RICK'S RACERS

	Balances at 1 July	
	Debit £	Credit £
Motor vehicles	24,200	
Plant and equipment	22,350	
Inventory	9,000	
Cash at bank	11,217	
Cash	150	
Sales ledger control	131,275	
Purchases ledger control		75,336
VAT owing to HM Revenue and Customs		15,127
Capital		26,247
Bank loan		12,500
Sales		276,132
Purchases	152,476	
Wages	35,465	
Motor expenses	3,617	
Repairs and renewals	2,103	
Rent and rates	3,283	
Light and heat	4,012	
Insurance	4,874	
Sundry expenses	1,320	
Suspense account (credit balance)		
Total	405,342	405,342

41   PERCY POTS

	Balances at 1 July	
	Debit £	Credit £
Motor vehicles	22,348	
Fixtures and fittings	9,234	
Inventory	4,800	
Bank		2,661
Petty cash	100	
Sales ledger control	61,025	
Purchases ledger control		35,275
VAT owing to HM Revenue and Customs		4,630
Capital		4,852
Sales		142,378
Sales returns	1,870	
Purchases	69,276	
Wages	13,500	
Motor expenses	873	
Office expenses	1,796	
Rent and rates	1,276	
Heat and light	1,022	
Insurance	1,629	
Miscellaneous expenses	1,047	
Suspense account		
Total	189,796	189,796

42   IVOR ISLAND

	Balances extracted on 30 April	Balances at 1 May	
		Debit £	Credit £
Motor vehicles	8,454	8,454	
Office building	28,676	28,676	
Inventory	15,369	15,369	
Bank	26,984	26,984	
Petty cash	459	459	
Sales ledger control	35,987	35,987	
Purchases ledger control	26,942		26,942
VAT (owing to HM Revenue and Customs)	231		(W1) 941
Capital	98,106		98,106
Sales	96,325		96,325
Sales returns	3,654		(W2) 3,954
Purchases	68,975	68,975	
Wages	18,564	18,564	
Motor expenses	1,269	1,269	
Office expenses	5,798	5,798	
Rates	4,300	4,300	
Heat and light	5,423	5,423	
Insurance	3,365	3,365	
Misc. expenses	2,645	2,645	
Suspense account (credit balance)	1,472	nil	nil
Totals		**226,268**	**226,268**

Workings:

(W1)

VAT

Details	Amount £	Details	Amount £
Balance b/f	231	Suspense	586
		Suspense	586
Balance c/d	941		
	1,172		**1,172**
		Balance b/d	941

(W2)

Sales returns

Details	Amount £	Details	Amount £
Suspense	2,256	Balance b/d	3,654
		Suspense	2,556
Balance c/d	3,954		
	6,210		**6,210**
		Balance b/d	3,954

43 RING OF ROSES

	Balances at 1 July	
	Debit £	Credit £
Motor vehicles	27,625	
Plant and equipment	5,000	
Inventory	7,350	
Cash at bank	14,345	
Cash	200	
Sales ledger control	121,275	
Purchases ledger control		67,323
VAT owing to HM Revenue and Customs		10,098
Capital		22,291
Sales		253,727
Sales returns	2,123	
Purchases	134,931	
Purchase returns		9,872
Wages	34,250	
Motor expenses	1,797	
Office expenses	4,946	
Rent and rates	2,321	
Heat and light	3,123	
Insurance	4,025	
Suspense account		
Total	363,311	363,311

44 HEARN

Journal entries

Account name	Debit £	Credit £
Rent	90	
Suspense		90
VAT	120	
Suspense		120

	Balances extracted on 30 June £	Balances at 1 July	
		Debit £	Credit £
Sales ledger control	34,560	34,560	
Purchases ledger control	21,420		21,420
VAT owing to HM Revenue and Customs	3,412		3,292
Capital	50,000		50,000
Sales	201,327		201,327
Sales returns	1,465	1,465	
Purchases	87,521	87,521	
Purchase returns	252		252
Plant and equipment	15,200	15,200	
Motor expenses	4,310	4,310	
Office expenses	10,321	10,321	
Rent and rates	21,420	21,510	
Heat and light	8,920	8,920	
Wages	53,205	53,205	
Irrecoverable debt	1,450	1,450	
Office equipment	42,030	42,030	
Bank overdraft	4201		4201
Suspense account (debit balance)	210		
Totals		**280,492**	**280,492**

45 RODMAN

Journal entries

Account name	Debit £	Credit £
Suspense	1,250	
VAT		1,250
Wages	8,600	
Suspense		8,600

	Balances extracted on 30 June £	Balances at 1 July	
		Debit £	Credit £
Sales ledger control	38,070	38,070	
Purchases ledger control	20,310		20,310
VAT owed from HM Revenue and Customs	2,510	1,260	
Capital	70,000		70,000
Sales	153,488		153,488
Sales returns	2,135	2,135	
Purchases	63,261	63,261	
Purchase returns	542		542
Plant and equipment	17,319	17,319	
Motor expenses	3,214	3,214	
Office expenses	6,421	6,421	
Rent and rates	17,414	17,414	
Heat and light	6,421	6,421	
Wages	45,532	54,132	
Irrecoverable debt	1,532	1,532	
Office equipment	35,313	35,313	
Bank overdraft	2,152		2,152
Suspense account (debit balance)	7,350		
Totals		**246,492**	**246,492**

UPDATE THE CASH BOOK

46   RIVERS LTD

(a) – (c)

Date 20XX	Details	Bank £	Date 20XX	Cheque number	Details	Bank £
01 June	Balance b/d	3,115	01 June	111013	Indigo beds	650
17 June	Bracken Ltd	300	01 June	111014	DirectFit	1,420
21 June	Airfleet Interiors	560	01 June	111015	Langdon	60
22 June	Harris Homes	333	01 June	111016	QPF Ltd	615
12 June	Ayreshire Build	970	02 June	111017	OMD Ltd	815
23 June	Bank interest	15	02 June	111018	Hamden Ltd	450
			13 June	111019	Freeman & Cope	522
			13 June		COLLINS	175
			20 June		Rent	500
			23 June		Bank charges	20
			23 June		Balance c/d	66
		5,293				5,293
24 June	Balance b/d	66				

47   LUXURY BATHROOMS

(a) – (c)

Date	Details	Bank	Date	Cheque	Details	Bank
01 April	Balance b/d	17,845	01 April	120045	R Sterling Ltd	8,850
19 April	Olsen & Lane	2,150	01 April	120046	Bert Cooper	2,250
22 April	Frith Ltd	685	01 April	120047	Hetko & Sons	64
22 April	Hodgetts & Co	282	02 April	120048	Barrett Ltd	3,256
04 April	Ricketts & Co	465	02 April	120049	K Plomer	542
			08 April	120050	I&E Brown	655
			08 April	120051	T Roberts	1,698
			14 April		AMB Ltd	2,265
			14 April		D Draper	2,950
			22 April		Bank charges	63
			23 April		Overdraft fee	25
24 April	Balance c/d	1,191				
		22,618				22,618
			25 April		Balance b/d	1,191

48   WHOLESALE FLOORING

(a) – (c)

Date 20XX	Details	Bank £	Date 20XX	Cheque number	Details	Bank £
			01 June		Balance b/d	5,125
16 June	Beeston's	550	01 June	104373	Good Iron	890
19 June	Airfleet exteriors	3,025	01 June	104374	Ashworth and Co	1,725
22 June	Jones's	2,775	01 June	104375	Ironfit	210
12 June	Aintree and Co	1,250	05 June	104376	OSS Ltd	1,275
			07 June	104377	Perfect Tools	725
			08 June	104378	Campden Ltd	784
			14 June	104379	Thornley and Thwaite	675
			14 June	104380	Castle and Cove	178
			20 June		MD County council	400
			23 June		Bank charges	160
23 June	Balance c/d	4,637	23 June		Overdraft fee	90
		12,237				12,237
			24 June		Balance b/d	4,637

49   24 HOUR TAXIS

(a) – (c)

Date 20XX	Details	Bank £	Date 20XX	Cheque number	Details	Bank £
01 June	Balance b/d	6,025	01 June	102597	Best Ideas	910
18 June	Earnshaw's	1,000	02 June	102598	Bentley and Burn	2,010
19 June	Mainstreet Ltd	1,206	02 June	102599	Bits and Bats	315
21 June	Housley Inc	1,725	03 June	102600	LPF Ltd	1,725
12 June	Barron Homes	1,475	07 June	102601	Essentials	686
			08 June	102602	Hopburn Ltd	675
			15 June	102603	Thistle Tools	410
			15 June	102604	C Campbell Ltd	275
			20 June		AB Insurance	1,250
			23 June		Bank charges	50
			23 June		Overdraft fee	25
			23 June		Balance c/d	3,100
		11,431				11,431
24 June	Balance b/d	3,100				

50   WOOD

(a) – (c)

Date 20XX	Details	Bank £	Date 20XX	Cheque number	Details	Bank £
01 June	Balance b/d	17,640				
03 June	Bradley	1,320	04 June	110341	Carr	1,540
03 June	Cash sales	9,420	04 June	110342	Ramsden	980
03 June	Thanoj	2,450	04 June	110343	Coulson	750
21 June	Cash sales	7,430	04 June	110344	Brodie	570
21 June	Devitt	1,990	04 June	110345	Jones	550
17 June	Interest earned	80	04 June	110346	Gritton	740
			20 June		Bore	250
			12 June		Southwell	820
			20 June		Direct debit Blundell	400
			23 June		Balance c/d	33,730
		40,330				**40,330**
24 June	Balance b/d	33,730				

51   PEARSON

(a) – (c)

Date 20XX	Details	Bank £	Date 20XX	Cheque number	Details	Bank £
01 June	Balance b/d	550	07 June	110123	Connell	430
09 June	Cash sales	840	07 June	110124	Renner	720
14 June	Cash sales	1,540	07 June	110125	Bond	750
22 June	Cunnington	1,730	07 June	110126	Hatton	75
02 June	Interest received	5	07 June	110127	Bull	270
			07 June	110128	Black	135
			07 June	110129	Southall	740
			02 June		McMenemy	1,200
			20 June		Findus	300
			23 June		Bank charges	25
			23 June		Balance c/d	20
		4,665				**4,665**
24 June	Balance b/d	20				

52 MCKEOWN

(a) – (c)

Date 20XX	Details	Bank £	Date 20XX	Cheque number	Details	Bank £
01 June	Balance b/d	7,180	07 June	110157	Williams	430
12 June	Sherwood	640	07 June	110158	Forecast	520
14 June	Cash sales	1,200	07 June	110159	Beasant	1,240
22 June	Tweedy	860	07 June	110160	Davison	1,420
23 June	Butterwood	440	07 June	110161	Mildenhall	750
01 June	Interest received	85	23 June		Wilmott	300
20 June	Coyne	1,630				
23 June	Interest received	35				
			23 June		Balance c/d	7,410
		12,070				12,070
24 June	Balance b/d	7,410				

BANK RECONCILIATIONS

53 RIVERS BANK RECONCILIATION

Balance per bank statement	£510
Add:	
Name: Airfleet Interiors	£560
Name: Harris Homes	£333
Total to add	**£893**
Less:	
Name: OMD Ltd	£815
Name: Freeman & Cope	£522
Total to subtract	**£1,337**
Balance as per cash book	**£66**

54 LUXURY BATHROOMS BANK RECONCILIATION

Balance per bank statement	**£82**
Add:	
Name: Frith Ltd	£685
Name: Hodgetts & Co	£282
Total to add	**£967**
Less:	
Name: K Plomer	£542
Name: T Roberts	£1,698
Total to subtract	**£2,240**
Balance as per cash book	**(£1,191)**

55 WHOLESALE FLOORING BANK RECONCILIATION

Balance per bank statement	**(£9,584)**
Add:	
Name: Airfleet Exteriors	£3,025
Name: Jones'	£2,775
Total to add	**£5,800**
Less:	
Name: Thornley & Thwaite	£675
Name: Castle & Cove	£178
Total to subtract	**£853**
Balance as per cash book	**(£4,637)**

56 24 HOUR TAXIS BANK RECONCILIATION

Balance per bank statement	**£854**
Add:	
Name: Mainstreet Ltd	£1,206
Name: Housley Inc	£1,725
Total to add	**£2,931**
Less:	
Name: Thistle Tools	£410
Name: C Campbell Ltd	£275
Total to subtract	**£685**
Balance as per cash book	**£3,100**

57   WOOD BANK RECONCILIATION

Balance per bank statement	£25,840
Add:	
Name: Cash sales	£7,430
Name: Devitt	£1,990
Total to add	£9,420
Less:	
Name: Ramsden	£980
Name: Jones	£550
Total to subtract	£1,530
Balance as per cash book	£33,730

58   PEARSON BANK RECONCILIATION

Balance per bank statement	(£105)
Add:	
Name: Cunnington	£1,730
Total to add	£1,730
Less:	
Name: Renner	£720
Name: Bond	£750
Name: Black	£135
Total to subtract	£1,605
Balance as per cash book	£20

(b) Show which security procedure listed below Pearson should use to ensure the security of receipts from customers.

	✓
Cash received from customers should be kept in a locked safe until banked	✓
Cash should be banked on a monthly basis	
Cheques received too late to bank should be posted through the bank's letter box	

59   MCKEOWN BANK RECONCILIATION

Balance per bank statement	**£8,770**
Add:	
Name: Tweedy	£860
Name: Butterwood	£440
Total to add	**£1,300**
Less:	
Name: Beasant	£1,240
Name: Davison	£1,420
Total to subtract	**£2,660**
Balance as per cash book	**£7,410**

(b) Show which security procedure listed below McKeown should use to ensure the security of receipts from customers.

	✓
Cash should be banked on a daily basis	✓
Cheques should be banked on a monthly basis	
Cheques received too late to bank should be posted through the bank's letter box	

PREPARE AND RECONCILE SALES/PURCHASE LEDGER CONTROL ACCOUNTS

60   MONSTER MUNCHIES

(a)

Details	Amount £	Debit ✓	Credit ✓
Balance of receivables at 1 June	48,000	✓	
Goods sold on credit	12,415	✓	
Receipts from credit customers	22,513		✓
Discount allowed	465		✓
Sales returns from credit customers	320		✓

(b)

Dr £37,117	✓

(c)

	£
Sales ledger control account balance as at 30 June	37,117
Total of subsidiary (sales) ledger accounts as at 30 June	36,797
Difference	320

(d)

Sales returns may have been omitted from the subsidiary ledger.	
Discounts allowed may have been omitted from the subsidiary ledger.	
Sales returns may have been entered in the subsidiary ledger twice.	✓
Discounts allowed may have been entered in the subsidiary ledger twice.	

(e)

Reconciliation of the sales ledger control account assures managers that the amount showing as owed to suppliers is correct.	
Reconciliation of the sales ledger control account assures managers that the amount showing as outstanding from customers is correct.	✓
Reconciliation of the sales ledger control account will show if a purchase invoice has been omitted from the purchase ledger.	
Reconciliation of the sales ledger control account will show if a purchase invoice has been omitted from the sales ledger.	

61 JACK'S BOX

(a)

Details	Amount £	Debit ✓	Credit ✓
Balance of receivables at 1 April	60,589	✓	
Goods sold on credit	26,869	✓	
Payments received from credit customers	29,411		✓
Discount allowed	598		✓
Goods returned from credit customers	1,223		✓

(b)

Dr £55,030	
Cr £55,030	
Dr £56,226	✓
Cr £56,226	
Dr £52,584	
Cr £52,584	

(c)

	£
Sales Ledger control account balances as at 30 April	56,226
Total of subsidiary (sales) ledger accounts as at 30 April	55,003
Difference	1,223

(d)

✓

Goods returned have been entered into the SLCA account twice.	
Discounts allowed have been omitted from the subsidiary ledger.	
Goods returned have been entered into the sales ledger twice.	✓
Discounts allowed have been entered into the SLCA twice.	

(e)

✓

Reconciliation of the sales ledger control account will show if a purchase invoice has been omitted from the purchases ledger.	
Reconciliation of the sales ledger control account will show if a sales invoice has been omitted from the purchases ledger.	
Reconciliation of the sales ledger control account assures managers that the amount showing due to suppliers is correct.	
Reconciliation of the sales ledger control account assures managers that the amount showing due from customers is correct.	✓

62 CILLA'S SINKS

(a)

Details	Amount £	Debit ✓	Credit ✓
Balance of payables at 1 June	52,150		✓
Goods bought on credit	19,215		✓
Payments made to credit suppliers	19,073	✓	
Discount received	284	✓	
Goods returned to credit suppliers	1,023	✓	

(b)

Cr £50,985	✓

(c)

	£
Purchase ledger control account balance as at 30 June	50,985
Total of subsidiary (purchase) ledger accounts as at 30 June	52,008
Difference	1,023

(d)

Goods returned may have been omitted from the subsidiary ledger.	✓
Discounts received may have been omitted from the subsidiary ledger.	
Goods returned may have been entered in the subsidiary ledger twice.	
Discounts received may have been entered into the subsidiary ledger twice.	

(e)

Reconciliation of the PLCA will help to identify any supplier invoices that have been omitted in error.	✓
Reconciliation of the purchase ledger control account will show if a sales invoice has been omitted from the purchase ledger.	
Reconciliation of the purchase ledger control account will show if a sales invoice has been omitted from the sales ledger.	
Reconciliation of the purchase ledger control account will help to identify any discounts allowed that have been omitted in error.	

63   VIK'S TRICKS

(a)

Details	Amount £	Debit ✓	Credit ✓
Balance of receivables at 1 June	58,120	✓	
Goods sold on credit	20,013	✓	
Receipts from credit customers	22,327		✓
Discount allowed	501		✓
Sales returns from credit customers	970		✓

(b)

Dr £54,335	✓

(c)

	£
Sales ledger control account balance as at 30 June	54,335
Total of subsidiary (sales) ledger accounts as at 30 June	55,305
Difference	970

(d)

Discounts allowed may have been entered in the subsidiary ledger twice.	
Discounts allowed may have been omitted from the subsidiary ledger.	
Sales returns may have been entered in the subsidiary ledger twice.	
Sales returns may have been omitted from the subsidiary ledger.	✓

(e)

Reconciliation of the sales ledger control account will help to identify any customer invoices that have been omitted in error.	✓
Reconciliation of the sales ledger control account will show if a purchase invoice has been omitted from the sales ledger.	
Reconciliation of the sales ledger control account will show if a purchase invoice has been omitted from the purchase ledger.	
Reconciliation of the sales ledger control account will help to identify any discounts received that have been omitted in error.	

64 ZHANG

SLCA

Details	Amount £	Details	Amount £
Balance b/d	65,830	SBD overcast	1,200
		Discount given	210
		Balance c/d	64,420
	65,830		**65,830**
Balance b/d	64,420		

List of balances:

	£
Total:	65,090
Contra missing	(800)
Credit note posted twice	130
Revised total:	64,420

(b)   **Show whether the following statements are true or false:**

	True ✓	False ✓
An aged trade receivables analysis is used when chasing customers for outstanding payments.	✓	
An aged trade receivables analysis is sent to credit customers when payments are being requested.		✓

65   HANDYSIDE

PLCA

Details	Amount £	Details	Amount £
Returns	120	Balance b/d	25,360
		Missing invoice	720
Balance c/d	25,960		
	26,080		**26,080**
		Balance b/d	25,960

List of balances:

	£
Total	26,000
Net amount entered	400
Returns	(350)
Transposition error	(90)
Revised total	25,960

(b)   **Show whether the following statements are true or false:**

	True ✓	False ✓
The purchases ledger control account enables a business to see how much is owed to individual suppliers		✓
The purchases ledger control account total should reconcile to the total of the list of supplier balances in the purchases ledger	✓	

VAT CONTROL ACCOUNT

66   BENJAMIN BISHOP

(a)

VAT control

Details	Amount £	Details	Amount £
Sales returns	640	Sales	37,600
Purchases	20,240	Cash sales	104
		Purchases returns	1,264
Balance c/d	18,088		
	38,968		**38,968**
		Balance b/d	18,088

(b)   Yes

67   RING RING TELEPHONE

(a)

VAT control

Details	Amount £	Details	Amount £
Sales returns	360	Sales	30,600
Purchases	16,200	Cash sales	48
		Purchases returns	1,160
Balance c/d	15,248		
	31,808		**31,808**
		Balance b/d	15,248

(b)   No – it is £15,248 owed **to** HMRC

68   JO'S JOINERS

(a)

VAT Control

Details	Amount £	Details	Amount £
Purchases	21,000	Sales	31,200
Sales returns	720	Cash sales	120
		Purchases returns	1,088
Balance c/d	10,688		
	32,408		**32,408**
		Balance b/d	10,688

(b)   Yes

69   PHILIP'S CABINS

(a)

VAT control

Details	Amount £	Details	Amount £
Sales returns	600	Sales	35,960
Purchases	20,040	Cash sales	112
		Purchases returns	1,144
Balance c/d	16,576		
	37,216		**37,216**
		Balance b/d	16,576

(b)   No – the amount owed to HMRC is £16,576.

70   DISLEY

	£	Debit	Credit
VAT total in the sales day book	65,420		65,420
VAT total in the purchases day book	21,340	21,340	
VAT total in the sales returns day book	480	480	
VAT balance brought forward, owed to HMRC	24,910		24,910
VAT on irrecoverable debts	830	830	
VAT on petty cash expenses paid	210	210	

(b)   No – the amount owed to HMRC is £67,470.

71 KERR

(a) **Show whether each item is a debit or credit balance by copying the amount into the correct column**

	£	Debit	Credit
VAT total in the purchase returns day book	1,320		1,320
VAT on cash purchases	2,670	2,670	
VAT on the sale of equipment	970		970
VAT refund received from HMRC	2,580		2,580
VAT on cash sales	5,680		5,680
VAT balance brought forward, due from HMRC	2,580	2,580	

(b) Yes – the amount owed is correct

72 NEILSON

	£	Debit	Credit
VAT total in the sales day book	54,670		54,670
VAT total in the purchases day book	26,340	26,340	
VAT total in the sales returns day book	1,240	1,240	
VAT total in the purchases returns day book	760		760
VAT on sale of equipment	3,210		3,210
VAT on petty cash expenses paid	500	500	
VAT balance brought forward, owed to HMRC	42,180		42,180
VAT on irrecoverable debts	430	430	
VAT paid to HMRC during the period	32,150	32,150	
VAT on cash sales	6,540		6,540
VAT on cash purchases	7,520	7,520	

(b) Yes – the amount owed is correct

THE BANKING SYSTEM

73 COLBECK

An organisation's document retention policy should contain a requirement for banking documents to be kept for a minimum of 7 years

False

A standing order will allow an organisation to make payments of fixed amounts

True

When a payment is made via cheque, the words on the cheque must match the amount shown in figures in order for the cheque to be valid.

True

Before accepting a cheque payment, an organisation should ask the bank if there are sufficient funds in the customer's bank account.

False

74 BLOSSOM BLOOMS

(a)

Checks to be made	Cheque	Telephone credit card payment
Check expiry date	✓	
Check issue number	✓	✓
Check not post dated		✓
Check security number	✓	
Check words and figures match		✓
Check card has not been tampered with	✓	✓

(b)

When Blossom Blooms makes payments to suppliers by debit card, the amount paid affects the bank current account

True

When Blossom Blooms makes payments to suppliers by credit card, the amount paid affects the bank current account

False

75 BELLA BAKERS

(a)

Service	Not offered by building societies ✓
Foreign currency	
Loan	
Overdraft	✓
Safe custody	✓
Savings account	
Telephone banking	

(b)

A bank cheque paid into a building society has to pass through the clearing system

True

A building society cheque paid into a bank has to pass through the clearing system

True

(c)

	✓
Aged receivable analysis	
Aged payable analysis	
Paying in slip stubs	✓
Credit cards	
Debit cards	
Bank Statements	✓
Cheque book stubs	✓
Customer invoices	

76 PETE'S PARROTS

(a)

Checks to be made	Cheque ✓	Telephone credit card payment ✓
Check expiry date		✓
Check issue number		
Check not posted dated	✓	
Check security number		✓
Check words and figures match	✓	
Check card has not been tampered with		

(b)

When Pete's Parrots makes payments to suppliers by credit card, the amount does not leave the bank current account immediately

True

When Pete's Parrots makes payments to suppliers by debit card, the amount paid affects the bank current account

True

77   BANKS

(a)

Service	Offered by BOTH banks & building societies ✓
Overdraft	
Savings account	✓
Foreign currency	✓
Safe custody	

(b)

	True ✓	False ✓
A building society cheque does not have to be passed to the bank of the issuer before the money becomes available.	✓	
A bank cheque paid into a building society has to pass through the clearing system.	✓	
A bank cheque does not have to be passed to the bank of the issuer before the money becomes available.		✓
A building society cheque paid into a bank has to pass through the clearing system.	✓	

(c)

	✓
Petty cash VAT invoices	
Cheque book stubs	✓
Supplier statement reconciliations	
Aged payables analysis	
Overdraft agreement	✓
Sales invoices	

78 KITE LTD

(a)

Checks to be made	BACS receipt ✓	Cheque ✓
Check security number		
Check remittance advice	✓	
Check crossed with 'Account Payee'		✓
Check payer is a customer	✓	
Check signature has been made		✓
Check card has not been tampered with		

(b)

	True ✓	False ✓
When Kite Ltd receives a remittance advice from a customer, the amount will already be in Kite Ltd's bank current account.		✓
When Kite Ltd makes a payment to a supplier by BACS, the amount paid affects the bank current account.	✓	

79 BUILDING SOCIETY

(a)

Service	Offered by building societies ✓
Foreign currency	✓
Loan	✓
Overdraft	
Safe custody	
Savings account	✓
Telephone banking	✓

(b)

A bank cheque paid into a building society does not have to pass through the clearing system

False

A building society cheque paid into a bank has to pass through the clearing system

True

A bank cheque has to be passed to the bank of the issuer before the money becomes available

True

A building society cheque does not have to be passed to the bank of the issuer before the money becomes available

True

(c)

	✓
Aged receivable analysis	
Aged payable analysis	
Cash book	
Credit cards	
Debit cards	
Bank statements	✓
Cheque book stubs	✓
Customer invoices	

80 GATES

(a)

Checks to be made	Cheque ✓	Telephone credit card payment ✓
Check expiry date	✓	
Check issue number	✓	✓
Check not post dated		✓
Check security number	✓	
Check words and figures match		✓
Check card has not been tampered with	✓	✓

(b)

When Gates makes payments to suppliers by credit card, the amount paid effects the bank current account

False

When Gates makes payments to suppliers by debit card, the amount paid affects the bank current account

True

81 METHODS OF PAYMENT

Match the payment need with the most likely method of payment to be used.

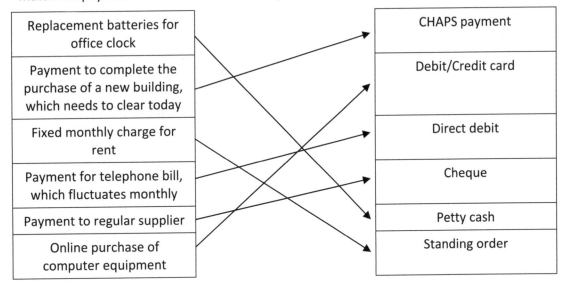

82 METHODS OF PAYMENT 2

Match the payment with the description below

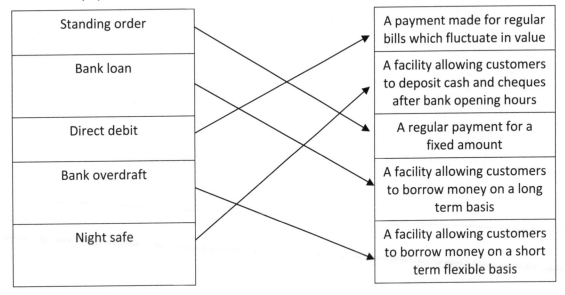

Section 3

MOCK ASSESSMENT QUESTIONS

TASK 1

Scott has started a new business, Scarn Ltd, and a new set of accounts are to be opened. A partially completed journal to record a selection of the opening entries is shown below.

Record the journal entries needed in the accounts in the general ledger of Scarn to deal with the opening entries.

Account name	Amount £	Debit ✓	Credit ✓
Cash at bank	7,250		
Bank loan	5,000		
Capital	10,625		
Motor vehicles	4,750		
Commission received	575		
Stationery	300		
Sundry expenses	225		
Discounts received	135		
Advertising	990		
Rent and rates	1,400		
Journal to record the opening entries of new business			

TASK 2

Beesley pays its employees by cheque every month and maintains a wages control account. A summary of last month's payroll transactions is shown below:

Item	£
Gross wages	26,500
Employers' NI	2,680
Employees' NI	2,760
Income tax	4,871
Employer pension contributions	1,000
Employee pension contributions	750

Record the journal entries needed in the general ledger to:

(i)   **Record the wages expense**

(ii)   **Record the HM Revenue and Customs liability**

(iii) **Record the net wages paid to the employees**

(iv)   **Record the Pension Liability**

(i)

Account name	Amount £	Debit ✔	Credit ✔

(ii)

Account name	Amount £	Debit ✔	Credit ✔

(iii)

Account name	Amount £	Debit ✔	Credit ✔

(iv)

Account name	Amount £	Debit ✔	Credit ✔

Picklist for each: Bank, Employees NI, Employers NI, HM Revenue and Customs, Income tax, Net wages, Pension, Trade Union, Wages control, Wages expense.

TASK 3

A credit customer, Halpert has ceased trading, owing Schrute £2,000 plus VAT

(a)   **Record the journal entries needed in the general ledger to write off Halpert's debt.**

Account name	Amount £	Debit ✔	Credit ✔

Select your account names from the following list: Schrute, Irrecoverable debts, Halpert, Purchases, Purchases ledger control, Sales, Sales ledger control, VAT.

(b)   **Show which of the errors below are, or are not, disclosed by the trial balance.**

Error in the general ledger	Error disclosed by the trial balance ✓	Error NOT disclosed by the trial balance ✓
Recording a bank payment for purchases on the debit side of both the bank and purchases account.		
Recording a payment for rent and rates in a non-current assets account.		
Recording a sales invoice in the sales account only.		
Incorrectly calculating the balance brought down on the rent account.		

(c)   **Show which error is an error of principle**

Error	✓
Recording a bank payment for office expenses on the debit side of the office furniture account.	
Recording a payment for motor expenses in the bank account, motor expenses account and miscellaneous expenses account.	
Recording a payment by cheque to a credit supplier in the bank account and purchases ledger control account only.	
Recording a cash payment for travel expenses in the cash account only.	

TASK 4

A payment of £15,600 for computer equipment has incorrectly been entered in the accounting records as £16,500.

(a)   **Record the journal entries needed in the general ledger to remove the incorrect entry**

Account name	Amount £	Debit ✓	Credit ✓

(b)   **Record the journal entries needed in the general ledger to record the correct entry**

Account name	Amount £	Debit ✓	Credit ✓

TASK 5

(a)   Bernard's trial balance was extracted and did not balance. The debit column of the trial balance totalled £109,798 and the credit column totalled £219,666.

What entry would be made in the suspense account to balance the trial balance?

Account name	Amount £	Debit ✓	Credit ✓

(b)   Hudson's initial trial balance includes a suspense account with a balance of £8,640.

The error has been traced to the purchase day-book shown below.

Purchase day-book

Date 20XX	Details	Invoice number	Total £	VAT £	Net £
30 Jun	Philbin	2,763	2,400	400	2,000
30 Jun	Lappin	2,764	3,120	520	2,600
30 Jun	Malone	2,765	4,080	680	3,400
	Totals		960	1,600	8,000

Identify the error and record the journal entries needed in the general ledger to:

(i)   **remove the incorrect entry**

(ii)   **record the correct entry**

(iii)   **remove the suspense account balance.**

(i)

Account name	Amount £	Debit ✓	Credit ✓

(ii)

Account name	Amount £	Debit ✓	Credit ✓

(iii)

Account name	Amount £	Debit ✓	Credit ✓

Picklist: Balance b/d, Purchases, Purchase ledger control account, VAT, Purchase returns, Suspense.

TASK 6

Kapoor's trial balance included a suspense account. All the bookkeeping errors have now been traced and the journal entries shown below have been recorded.

Journal entries

Account name	Debit £	Credit £
Office expenses		632
Suspense	632	
Repairs	873	
Suspense		873
Loan interest expense	962	
Bank interest received		962

Post the journal entries to the general ledger accounts. Dates are not required.

Office expenses

Details	Amount £	Details	Amount £

Repairs

Details	Amount £	Details	Amount £

Suspense

Details	Amount £	Details	Amount £
Balance b/d	241		

Loan interest expense

Details	Amount £	Details	Amount £

Bank interest received

Details	Amount £	Details	Amount £

Picklist: Balance b/d, Bank interest received, Loan interest expense, Bank interest paid, Office expenses, Repairs, Suspense.

TASK 7

On 31 March, Howard extracted an initial trial balance which did not balance, and a suspense account was opened. On 1 April journal entries were prepared to correct the errors that had been found, and clear the suspense account. The list of balances in the initial trial balance, and the journal entries to correct the errors, are shown below.

Re-draft the trial balance by placing the figures in the debit or credit column. You should take into account the journal entries which will clear the suspense account.

	Balances extracted on 31 March	Balances at 1 April	
		Debit £	Credit £
Sales	190,029		
Purchases	104,698		
Admin expenses	1,209		
Irrecoverable debt expense	150		
Sales ledger control account	28,200		
Discounts allowed	4,090		
Purchases ledger control account	18,929		
Sales tax (VAT) owing to tax authorities	10,000		
Bank interest paid	300		
Bank loan	16,700		
Fixtures and fittings	43,000		
Computer equipment	11,111		
Motor vehicles at cost	4,567		

Motor expenses	142		
Discounts received	132		
Rent and rates	1,678		
Light and heat	980		
Entertainment expense	120		
Sundry expenses	85		
Suspense account (debit balance)	35,460		

Journal entries:

Account name	Debit £	Credit £
Suspense		20,000
Sales ledger control account	20,000	

Account name	Debit £	Credit £
Bank loan	15,460	
Suspense		15,460

TASK 8

On 28 April Dunder Mifflin received the following bank statement as at 24 April.

SKB Bank plc
68 London Road, Reading, RG8 4RN

To: Dunder Mifflin	Account No: 55548921		24 April 20XX	
	Statement of Account			

Date 20XX	Detail	Paid out £	Paid in £	Balance £
03 April	Balance b/d			18,000 C
03 April	Cheque 120045	6,234		11,766 C
04 April	Bank Giro Prince Paper		342	12,108 C
04 April	Cheque 120046	1,632		10,476 C
05 April	Cheque 120047	41		10,435 C
08 April	Cheque 120048	4,444		5,991 C
14 April	Direct debit Staples Ltd	2,878		3,113 C
14 April	Direct debit Steamtown Mall	2,865		248 C
14 April	Cheque 120050	432		184 D
22 April	Paid in at SKB Bank		5,321	5,137 C
22 April	Bank charges	54		5,083 C
23 April	Overdraft fee	27		5,056 C
	D = Debit C = Credit			

The cash book as at 24 April is shown below.

Cash Book

Date	Details	Bank	Date	Cheque	Details	Bank
01 April	Balance b/d	18,000	01 April	120045	Mose Ltd	6,234
19 April	Wallace	5,321	01 April	120046	Sabre	1,632
22 April	Bennett	685	01 April	120047	Hannan	41
22 April	Lewis	282	02 April	120048	Flinderson	4,444
			02 April	120049	Bratton	542
			08 April	120050	Flax	432
			08 April	120051	Vickers	1,698
			14 April		Staples	2,878

Details column options: Balance b/d, balance c/d, Bank charges, Mose Ltd, Sabre, Hannan, Steamtown Mall, Flinderson, Bratton, Flax, Vickers, Wallace, Bennett, Lewis, Prince Paper, Opening balance, Overdraft fees, <empty>

(a)   **Check the items on the bank statement against the items in the cash book.**

(b)   **Enter any items in the cash book as needed.**

(c)   **Total the cash book and clearly show the balance carried down at 24 April (closing balance) and brought down at 25 April (opening balance).**

TASK 9

On 28 June Martinez Ltd received the following bank statement as at 23 June.

<table>
<tr><td colspan="6" align="center">**Four Kings Bank PLC**</td></tr>
<tr><td colspan="6" align="center">**124 Four Kings Way, Newton Mearns, GL10 5QR**</td></tr>
<tr><td colspan="2">To: Martinez Ltd</td><td colspan="2" align="center">Account No: 16135844</td><td colspan="2" align="center">23 June 20XX</td></tr>
<tr><td colspan="6" align="center">**Statement of Account**</td></tr>
<tr><td>Date</td><td>Detail</td><td>Paid out</td><td>Paid in</td><td colspan="2">Balance</td></tr>
<tr><td>20XX</td><td></td><td>£</td><td>£</td><td colspan="2">£</td></tr>
<tr><td>04 June</td><td>Balance b/d</td><td></td><td></td><td>6,025</td><td>C</td></tr>
<tr><td>05 June</td><td>Cheque 102597</td><td>910</td><td></td><td>5,115</td><td>C</td></tr>
<tr><td>05 June</td><td>Cheque 102598</td><td>2,010</td><td></td><td>3,105</td><td>C</td></tr>
<tr><td>05 June</td><td>Cheque 102599</td><td>315</td><td></td><td>2,790</td><td>C</td></tr>
<tr><td>11 June</td><td>Cheque 102602</td><td>675</td><td></td><td>2,115</td><td>C</td></tr>
<tr><td>12 June</td><td>Bank Giro credit California</td><td></td><td>1,475</td><td>3,590</td><td>C</td></tr>
<tr><td>13 June</td><td>Cheque 102600</td><td>1,725</td><td></td><td>1,865</td><td>C</td></tr>
<tr><td>15 June</td><td>Cheque 102601</td><td>686</td><td></td><td>1,179</td><td>C</td></tr>
<tr><td>19 June</td><td>Paid in at Four Kings Bank</td><td></td><td>1,000</td><td>2,179</td><td>C</td></tr>
<tr><td>20 June</td><td>Direct debit AB Insurance</td><td>1,250</td><td></td><td>929</td><td>C</td></tr>
<tr><td>23 June</td><td>Bank charges</td><td>50</td><td></td><td>879</td><td>C</td></tr>
<tr><td>23 June</td><td>Overdraft fee</td><td>25</td><td></td><td>854</td><td>C</td></tr>
<tr><td colspan="6" align="center">D = Debit   C = Credit</td></tr>
</table>

The cash book is seen below:

Date 20XX	Details	Bank £	Date 20XX	Cheque number	Details	Bank £
01 June	Balance b/d	6,025	01 June	102597	Cordray	910
18 June	Martin	1,000	02 June	102598	Palmer	2,010
19 June	Packer Ltd	1,206	02 June	102599	Filippelli	315
21 June	Miner Ltd	1,725	03 June	102600	Anderson Ltd	1,725
12 June	Robert California	1,475	07 June	102601	Brent	686
			08 June	102602	Poor Richard's Ltd	675
			15 June	102603	D'Angelo	410
			15 June	102604	Klump	275
			20 June		Ping Ltd	1,250
			23 June		Bank charges	50
			23 June		Overdraft fee	25
			23 June		Balance c/d	3,100
		11,431				11,431
24 June	Balance b/d	3,100				

Complete the bank reconciliation statement as at 23 June.

Bank reconciliation statement as at 23 June

Balance per bank statement	£
Add:	
Name:	£
Name:	£
Total to add	£
Less:	
Name:	£
Name:	£
Total to subtract	£
Balance as per cash book	£

Name options: Ping Ltd, D'Angelo, Klump, Brent, Poor Richard's Ltd, Anderson Ltd, Filippelli, Palmer, Cordray, Robert California, Miner, Packer, Martin.

TASK 10

This is a summary of transactions with suppliers of Wuph during the month of May.

(a) **Show whether each entry will be a debit or credit in the purchases ledger control account in the general ledger.**

Details	Amount £	Debit ✓	Credit ✓
Balance of payables at 1 May	89,726		
Credit purchases	62,362		
Cheque payments to payables	87,251		
Discounts received	11,928		
Returns outwards	12,987		

(b) **What will be the balance brought down on 1 May on the above account?**

	✓
Dr £ 49,804	
Cr £ 49,804	
Dr £ 39,922	
Cr £ 39,922	
Dr £ 65,896	
Cr £ 65,896	

(c) The following credit balances were in the purchases ledger on 1 June.

	£
DMI	8,336
Ronnie's	7,361
Cynthia	9,101
Roy's Ltd	9,872
Goldenface	4,321
Levenson	12,859

Reconcile the balances shown above with the sales ledger control account balance you have calculated in part (a).

	£
Purchase ledger control account balance as at 1 June	
Total of purchase ledger accounts as at 30 June	
Difference	

(d)   **What may have caused the difference you calculated in part (c)?**

	✓
Goods returned may have been entered in the purchases ledger twice from the purchases ledger.	
Discounts received may have been entered in the purchases ledger twice.	
Discounts received may have been omitted from the purchases ledger control account.	
Discounts received may have been omitted from the purchases ledger.	

(e)   It is important to reconcile the purchases ledger control account on a regular basis.

Which of the following statements is true?

	✓
Reconciliation of the purchases ledger control account assures managers that the amount showing as outstanding to customers is correct.	
Reconciliation of the purchases ledger control account assures managers that the amount showing as outstanding from suppliers is correct.	
Reconciliation of the purchases ledger control account assures managers that the amount showing as outstanding to suppliers is correct.	
Reconciliation of the purchases ledger control account will show if a purchase invoice has been omitted from the purchases ledger.	

TASK 11

	£
VAT owing from HM Revenue and Customs at 1 June	16,750
VAT total in the purchases day book	23,450
VAT total in the sales day book	46,750
VAT total in the purchases returns day book	230
VAT total in the sales returns day book	870
VAT on cash sales	3,450
VAT on petty cash payments	70
VAT refund received from HM Revenue and Customs	6,430
VAT on irrecoverable debts written off	640
VAT on the sale of office equipment	1,230

Show how each of the transactions would be recorded in the VAT control account by entering items into the appropriate side of the control account, stating whether the balance is owed to HMRC or recoverable from HMRC.

VAT control

Details	Amount £	Details	Amount £

Picklist: Balance b/d, Balance c/d, Sales, Purchases, Sales returns, Purchase returns, Cash sales, VAT refund, Irrecoverable debts, Office equipment sold

TASK 12

(a) State whether the items below are true or false.

	True ✓	False ✓
A direct debit is an instruction to a customer's bank to make regular payments, which are usually of a fixed amount.		
A cheque is considered to be 'out of date', 7 months past the date of the cheque.		
The drawer of a cheque is the account holder who is making the payment.		

(b) Identify which checks should be done on the payment types identified below

Checks to be made	Cheque ✓	Telephone credit card payment ✓	Neither ✓
Check expiry date			
Check issue number			
Check not post dated			
Check security number			
Check words and figures match			
Check card has not been tampered with			

(c)   **State whether the items below are true or false**

	True ✓	False ✓
When Gates makes payments to suppliers by credit card, the amount paid affects the bank current account.		
When Gates makes payments to suppliers by debit card, the amount paid affects the bank current account.		
A cheque payment does not appear on the bank statement.		
An unpresented cheque is a cheque payment that has cleared the bank prior to the reconciliation of the bank being performed.		

Section 4

MOCK ASSESSMENT ANSWERS

TASK 1

Account name	Amount £	Debit ✓	Credit ✓
Cash at bank	7,250	✓	
Bank loan	5,000		✓
Capital	10,625		✓
Motor vehicles	4,750	✓	
Commission received	575		✓
Stationery	300	✓	
Sundry expenses	225	✓	
Discounts received	135		✓
Advertising	990	✓	
Rent and rates	1,400	✓	
Journal to record the opening entries of new business			

TASK 2

(i)

Account name	Amount £	Debit ✓	Credit ✓
Wages expense	30,180	✓	
Wages control	30,180		✓

(ii)

Account name	Amount £	Debit ✓	Credit ✓
HM Revenue and Customs	10,311		✓
Wages control	10,311	✓	

(iii)

Account name	Amount £	Debit ✓	Credit ✓
Bank	18,119		✓
Wages control	18,119	✓	

(iv)

Account name	Amount £	Debit ✓	Credit ✓
Pension	1,750		✓
Wages control	1,750	✓	

TASK 3

(a)

Account name	Amount £	Debit ✓	Credit ✓
Irrecoverable debt expense	2,000	✓	
VAT	400	✓	
Sales ledger control account	2,400		✓

(b)

Error in the general ledger	Error disclosed by the trial balance ✓	Error NOT disclosed by the trial balance ✓
Recording a bank payment for purchases on the debit side of both the bank and purchases account.	✓	
Recording a payment for rent and rates in a non-current assets account.		✓
Recording a sales invoice in the sales account only.	✓	
Incorrectly calculating the balance brought down on the rent account.	✓	

(c)

Error	✓
Recording a bank payment for office expenses on the debit side of the office furniture account.	✓
Recording a payment for motor expenses in the bank account, motor expenses account and miscellaneous expenses account.	
Recording a payment by cheque to a credit supplier in the bank account and purchases ledger control account only.	
Recording a cash payment for travel expenses in the cash account only.	

TASK 4

(a)

Account name	Amount £	Debit ✓	Credit ✓
Bank	16,500	✓	
Computer equipment	16,500		✓

(b)

Account name	Amount £	Debit ✓	Credit ✓
Bank	15,600		✓
Computer equipment	15,600	✓	

TASK 5

(a)

Account name	Amount £	Debit ✓	Credit ✓
Suspense	109,868	✓	

(b)   (i)

Account name	Amount £	Debit ✓	Credit ✓
Purchase ledger control account	960	✓	

(ii)

Account name	Amount £	Debit ✓	Credit ✓
Purchase ledger control account	9,600		✓

(iii)

Account name	Amount £	Debit ✓	Credit ✓
Suspense	8,640	✓	

TASK 6

Office expenses

Details	Amount £	Details	Amount £
		Suspense	632

Repairs

Details	Amount £	Details	Amount £
Suspense	873		

Suspense

Details	Amount £	Details	Amount £
Balance b/d	241	Repairs	873
Office expenses	632		

Loan interest expense

Details	Amount £	Details	Amount £
Bank interest received	962		

Bank interest received

Details	Amount £	Details	Amount £
		Loan interest expense	962

TASK 7

	Balances extracted on 31 March	Balances at 1 April	
		Debit £	Credit £
Sales	190,029		190,029
Purchases	104,698	104,698	
Admin expenses	1,209	1,209	
150	150		
48,200	28,200		
Discounts allowed	4,090	4,090	
Purchases ledger control account	18,929		18,929
Sales tax (VAT) owing to tax authorities	10,000		10,000
Bank interest paid	300	300	
Bank loan	16,700		1,240
Fixtures and fittings	43,000	43,000	
Computer equipment	11,111	11,111	
Motor vehicles at cost	4,567	4,567	
Motor expenses	142	142	
Discounts received	132		132
Rent and rates	1,678	1,678	
Light and heat	980	980	
Entertainment expense	120	120	
Sundry expenses	85	85	
Suspense account (debit balance)	35,460		
Totals		**220,330**	**220,330**

TASK 8

Date	Details	Bank	Date	Cheque	Details	Bank
01 April	Balance b/d	18,000	01 April	120045	Mose Ltd	6,234
19 April	Wallace	5,321	01 April	120046	Sabre	1,632
22 April	Bennett	685	01 April	120047	Hannan	41
22 April	Lewis	282	02 April	120048	Flinderson	4,444
4 April	**Prince Paper**	**342**	02 April	120049	Bratton	542
			08 April	120050	Flax	432
			08 April	120051	Vickers	1,698
			14 April		Staples	2,878
			14 April		**Steamtown Mall**	**2,865**
			22 April		**Bank charges**	**54**
			23 April		**Overdraft fee**	**27**
			24 April		Balance c/d	3,783
		24,630				**24,630**
24 April	Balance b/d	3,783				

TASK 9

Bank reconciliation statement as at 23 April 20XX

	£	£
Balance per bank statement		854
Add:		
Name: Packer Ltd	1,206	
Name: Miner Ltd	1,725	
	———	
Total to add		2,931
Less:		
Name: D'Angelo	410	
Name: Klump	275	
	———	
Total to subtract		685
		———
Balance as per cash book		3,100

TASK 10

(a)   **Purchase ledger control account**

Details	Amount £	Debit ✓	Credit ✓
Balance of payables at 1 May	89,726		✓
Credit purchases	62,362		✓
Cheque payments to payables	87,251	✓	
Discounts received	11,928	✓	
Returns outwards	12,987	✓	

(b)   Balance b/d = Credit balance £39,922

(c)   **Reconciliation**

	£
Purchases ledger control account balance as at 1 June	39,922
Total of purchases ledger accounts as at 1 June	51,850
Difference	11,928

(d)   **Cause of difference**

= Discounts received may have been omitted from the purchases ledger

(e)   **The true statement is:**

Reconciliation of the purchases ledger control account assures managers that the amount showing as outstanding to suppliers is correct.

TASK 11

VAT control

Details	Amount £	Details	Amount £
Balance b/d	16,750	Sales	46,750
Puchases	23,450	Purchase returns	230
Sales returns	870	Cash sales	3,450
Petty cash	70	VAT refund	6,430
Irrecoverable debts	640	Office equipment sold	1,230
Balance c/d	16,310		
	58,090		**58,090**
		Balance b/d	16,310

The balance is owed to HMRC as a liability of £16,310.

TASK 12

(a)

	True ✓	False ✓
A direct debit is an instruction to a customer's bank to make regular payments, which are usually of a fixed amount.		✓
A cheque is considered to be 'out of date', 7 months past the date of the cheque.	✓	
The drawer of a cheque is the account holder who is making the payment.	✓	

(b)

Checks to be made	Cheque ✓	Telephone credit card payment ✓	Neither ✓
Check expiry date		✓	
Check issue number			✓
Check not post dated	✓		
Check security number		✓	
Check words and figures match	✓		
Check card has not been tampered with			✓

(c)

	True ✓	False ✓
When Gates makes payments to suppliers by credit card, the amount paid effects the bank current account.		✓
When Gates makes payments to suppliers by debit card, the amount paid affects the bank current account.	✓	
A cheque payment does not appear on the bank statement.		✓
An unpresented cheque is a cheque payment that has cleared the bank prior to the reconciliation of the bank being performed.		✓